BUSINESS NEGOTIATION

BUSINESS NEGOTIATION

A PRACTICAL WORKBOOK

Paul T. Steele
and
Tom Beasor

GOWER

Published by
Gower Publishing Limited
Gower House
Croft Road
Aldershot
Hampshire GU11 3HR
England

Gower Publishing Company
Suite 420
101 Cherry Street
Burlington, 05401-4405
USA

Reprinted 2002, 2005

Paul Steele and Tom Beasor have asserted their right under the Copyright, Designs
and Patents Act 1988 to be identified as the authors of this work.

British Library Cataloguing in Publication Data
Steele, Paul
Business negotiation : a practical workbook
1.Negotiation in business
I.Title II.Beasor, Tom
658.4'052

ISBN 0 566 08072 9

Library of Congress Cataloging-in-Publication Data
Steele, Paul, 1947–
    Business negotiation : a practical workbook / Paul T. Steele and
  Tom Beasor.
      p. cm.
    Includes index.
    ISBN 0–566–08072–9
    1. Negotiation in business.   I. Beasor, Tom, 1951–   .
  II. Title.
  HD58.6.S738   1999
  658.4'052--dc21   98-33379
                                                          CIP

Typeset in 10 point Plantin Light by Wileman Design
and printed in Great Britain by MPG BOOKS Ltd, Bodmin.

CONTENTS

ACKNOWLEDGEMENTS

Where do good ideas come from? How many of us can reasonably claim that something new was all our own work?

Most new concepts come from the amalgam that is our experience, our own creativity and the seeds that others sow for us to germinate. Environments that are conducive to the flourishing of such ideas are precious places and in such places new ways of managing evolve.

PMMS Consulting Group is such a place, and we have been fortunate to share in the riches of such an environment. We were stimulated by many forward-thinking individuals to produce this workbook. The concepts in it owe their origins to so many people that it is impossible to acknowledge them all individually. We are particularly indebted to negotiating specialists working within the PMMS team.

We acknowledge the contributions from our many clients ranging from the largest multinational to modest-sized private companies who have ensured that our concepts have an immediate payback and practical application in the world of commercial negotiation. Without them there would be no purpose.

To all our colleagues and clients, our sincere thanks. We regret we cannot acknowledge each individually. However, it is possible to recognize some specific contributions: David S. Wood for his reasoned contributions and in-depth practical knowledge; Paul E. Rogers for many creative hours spent mainly with Tom Beasor developing new models for commercial relationships and interpreting them into better negotiation concepts; R. Ian Patterson for his voracious reading and contributions to drafts of the workbook; Emma Hill and Sue Swindlehurst for their hard work word-processing and laying out the handbook from our original manuscript; and finally, Barry J. Hankinson for his constructive criticisms, and his proofing of the work and finalising the many details needed to bring the book to fruition.

Some of the ideas discussed in this workbook first appeared in *It's a Deal* by Paul Steele, John Murphy and Richard Russill (McGraw-Hill, 1989).

Paul T. Steele   Tom Beasor

PMMS Consulting Group
15 Church Road
Lytham
FY8 2EL
England

INTRODUCTION

This workbook has been written to provide the readers with both a stimulating medium for the discussion of key negotiation topics and a means to equip themselves confidently with techniques for implementing them. It is designed to be a practical guide for those readers who wish to be confident and competent practitioners. It is very much a users' book.

WHO SHOULD USE IT?

The book is designed as a standard textbook for those who wish to understand the subject better but, more significantly, it is a means by which the reader can develop effective techniques to put that knowledge into practice.

Newcomers to negotiation will find simple integrated sections that will help them move through the subject in easy supportive steps. The 'voice' of the tutor will be with you as you study. Practical application of skills will be the main objective.

Experienced teachers and learners will find the exercises of real practical value for understanding 'how' and 'why' people behave the way they do. We have designed this book with a practical 'how to' bias and those learning on their own will find an easy progression along a path of 20 steps towards increased negotiation competence.

Many experienced negotiators will be interested to compare their views with ours on the resolving of negotiation dilemmas.

HOW IT IS STRUCTURED

Part 1 is a discussion of the basics of negotiation. It is designed to provide an answer to three key questions:

- Chapter 1 asks, 'Negotiation – what is it?'
- Chapter 2 asks, 'What is the most appropriate relationship?'
- Chapter 3 asks, 'Which style of negotiation is the most effective?'

This section gives the reader a solid foundation of theory on which to base the practical tools that we offer in Part 2.

Part 2 is in four sections:

- Chapter 4 looks at objective setting and planning.
- Chapter 5 covers the first phases in a negotiation.
- Chapter 6 gives advice on managing movement.
- Chapter 7 provides help on other aspects of negotiation.

We have organised this part so that each chapter is divided into a series of steps. Each step has a standardised format:

- There is always a discussion of a major topic. We then ensure that you are 'match fit' for putting the topic into practice.
- We provide scripts for each step to help you find the correct turn of phrase and tone.
- We then look at some tactics and counterplays that are relevant to that issue.
- This is followed by a practical exercise that will keep the workbook relevant to negotiations in your business and personal life.
- Negotiation dilemmas are found in each step to put the theory into a practical context. These are accompanied by our opinion on how they can be best resolved.
- Each step ends by asking you to revisit the key learning points and encouraging you to make a real commitment to action.

We hope that this book will stimulate you to examine your current style and technique and find ways to reach more successful outcomes, create better business relationships and take pride in your enhanced performance.

PART 1

INTRODUCTION TO NEGOTIATION

1 NEGOTIATION – WHAT IS IT?

We recognize the skill with which an experienced helmsman negotiates a busy harbour to tie up, being mindful of charted hidden dangers and the unpredictability of the behaviour of other users. But are we always aware that we should be exercising a similar degree of skill and attention to detail in handling our interpersonal relationships? Statistics on the rising trend of divorce make for grim analysis of most domestic scenes, but are we any better equipped to deal with commercial difficulties? We doubt it, if only because the nature of negotiation and the impact it has on relationships has yet to be widely understood. All too often we see people exchange information, test understanding and then make a decision – *and believe they have negotiated*. Well, they haven't.

NEGOTIATION DEFINED

Using a workable definition, we see negotiation as

> **A process through which parties *move*
> from their initially divergent positions
> to a point where agreement may be
> reached.**

Let us examine negotiation from a practical viewpoint using it in an everyday example:

> *The compact disc player*
> A couple bought a CD player from a well-known electronic goods stockist located out of town. They travelled home some miles away. Following the manufacturer's instructions carefully, they set it up and plugged it in. It was lifeless. A phone call to the stockist elicited a typically brusque response: 'Bring it in and we will see what can be done about it.'

Any summary of this opening scenario would be incomplete if it failed to identify customer dissatisfaction and a potential for a marked difference of opinion between the parties:

> Having reflected on the irony of being invited to spend more in order to obtain a reliable product, the customer rang the sales manager with a number of observations:
>
> - A separate return journey was inconvenient.
> - Time lost could profitably be spent elsewhere.
> - There were costs for petrol and parking which would be eliminated if the retailer collected.
> - There would be loss of goodwill if the matter was not resolved satisfactorily.
>
> The sales manager was somewhat taken aback. It was not normal custom and practice to reimburse costs.
>
> The customer, sensing the Manager's hesitation, pressed his point and said a set of classical CDs and a box of VHS tapes would be an acceptable recompense.
> In due course the customer called in at his convenience and collected a new CD player, which was unboxed, fully tested and reboxed in his presence, along with a gift-wrapped parcel of high quality discs and tapes accompanied by a letter of apology. The customer went away satisfied with the outcome and still frequents the shop.

Points to Ponder

Jot down your initial reaction to these points.

1. As the customer how would you have proceeded differently?

2. When did the negotiation actually begin?

3. Do you think the customer's demands were aimed too high? What would you have asked for?

4. What behavioural approach did the customer use?

5. What other methods could the customer have effectively employed?

6. Do you think parity has been satisfactorily restored between the parties to their mutual satisfaction?

OUR VIEW

1. In asking this question we are concerned with intuitively identifying and exploring possible alternative styles of approach that could have been adopted. We are looking at high and stretching objectives but ones that maintain our credibility. We are also aiming to provide ourselves with the widest choice of options depending on both the commercial opportunities and the different people involved.

    The buyer has done well to avoid putting 'markers' down by refraining from setting an upper limit on what can be achieved. A 'marker' is usually a figure – a price, a delivery period, a number of days holiday – that is your ideal position in any negotiation. By putting a marker down you immediately put a ceiling on what you can achieve, and you could prevent the other party moving further in your favour.

    In this example a mixture of logic, used with low key emotion, has yielded a satisfactory beginning.

2. If you have to ask yourself when a negotiation started then you can almost certainly be sure that you are too late. A negotiation begins at the very first point at which either party has the opportunity to influence the other. It could have begun with a letter or might have started even earlier. Many customers will have been influenced by the store's reputation or advertising.

3. Aiming high allows room for manoeuvre. Incremental adjustments can favourably influence the atmosphere and actions of the other party. Aim as high as possible. Research indicates that those people who ask for more, gain more. However, do not take up a position so extreme as to damage your credibility.

4. Whereas logic was clearly evident, there was a hint of a more emotive appeal which could have been based on customers' rights had the stockist not been amenable to reason.

5. Discreet threat can be employed in circumstances where power is seen to best serve the interests of the party resorting to it. When one party has leverage there is always a temptation to use it. Applied skilfully, this is a very legitimate approach. Conducted poorly, such coercion is seen as overpowering and destructive.

It is better to use brains before brawn. Heavy handed threats have a tendency to backfire on you, particularly when used against parties whose cooperation you may need at some point in the future.

Another approach, much in favour in Anglo-Saxon culture, would have been to use compromise. It differs from bargaining in that it applies to reaching an understanding on a single issue by agreeing to a satisfactory midpoint. A willingness to compromise could be a sign of potential weakness and the customer avoided this approach by the use of several different variables. Compromise when used in Anglo-Saxon culture denotes a desire to 'split the difference'. We believe that this should be a tactic of last resort and should remain at the tail end of the negotiator's repertoire.

6. This has to be a matter for both parties. Each will have had their own objectives and each will be seeking a different outcome. It is not a sign of weakness that a negotiator is dissatisfied with the outcome. Experienced negotiators are always trying to drain the last drop from every deal.

This example of negotiation over a CD player provides a basis for exploring two further considerations that play a part in better understanding the subject:

- The kind of relationship being sought (this is discussed further in Chapter 2).
- The style of negotiation that comes most naturally to us (this is analysed in depth in Chapter 3).

NEGOTIATING FREQUENCY – IN THE SHORT AND LONG TERM

Let's ask ourselves what we are considering – a date or a marriage!

- Will it be an open/shut instance for which a single meeting should suffice?
- Is it a more complex matter which may possibly take several meetings to resolve because long-term interests are involved?

Having decided the frequency of relationship, the next task is to evaluate the merits of the business arrangement best suited to meeting the perceived objective of both parties, and the style of approach to match. In the CD player negotiation the shop manager is interested in a long term relationship (i.e. a regular customer); the customer may also want this.

THE PROCESS

Negotiation is a process through which parties move from their initially divergent positions to a point where agreement may be reached.

The five main approaches to negotiation are:

- compromise
- bargaining
- threat
- emotion
- logical reasoning.

All five approaches share a common purpose – to achieve sufficient movement by parties to reach agreement. They can be used in isolation – or in combination – to achieve their purpose.

Cultures throughout the world have their own individual means of achieving movement from the other party. In Britain many show a preference for compromise, whereas it has been noted that the countries of Eastern Europe and the Far East tend more to use emotion and threat. The Germans are renowned for employing logical reasoning and the Americans enjoy bargaining.

These cultural generalizations provide only a rough guide. National stereotypes do a grave injustice to skilled negotiators of any nationality capable of a wider range of techniques and approaches.

A negotiation can be regarded as a ritual, attracting procedural nuances which may call for careful compliance. If the process happens too quickly there is a risk of one of the participants feeling dissatisfied. They are likely to feel they could have done better had they been more adventurous in setting their planned limits. The feeling that a good contract cannot be agreed without a contest may appear illogical but can be true nevertheless. Appearance (or 'face', in an Eastern culture) is all-important.

Experienced negotiators understand these key elements of human nature:

- We like to appear to be popular.
- We wish to avoid losing prestige (face).

- We will offer concessions at little cost to ourselves ('straw issues') at the concluding stage of a difficult negotiation in order to finalize the deal and make the other party feel better.
- Emotional factors carry as much weight as any single factual component in the careful planning of a negotiation.

KEY POINTS

1. Negotiation is all about creating a movement between parties with initially divergent positions.
2. The negotiation process is one of interaction between parties with differing objectives which can be resolved by a *variety* of approaches.
3. Avoid gaining a reputation for using only one approach when attempting to move another party to your way of thinking.
4. Both parties could use emotion. Be prepared for behaviour that could upset your logically sound plan.
5. Avoid putting 'markers' down which limit your flexibility.
6. Before you use threat think about the consequences. Negotiators are ordinary people who don't easily forget being threatened. Given the opportunity they will get their own back, so don't go over the top.
7. Engineer sufficient reassurance into the outcome to ensure that the other party think honour has been satisfied – a particularly significant point should you have to negotiate with the other party on another occasion.

What's next?

Now that you appreciate the nature of negotiation it is timely to consider the kind of relationship the differing parties would like to establish. Write down quickly before you move on what types of relationship you might seek with the other party in a negotiation.

2 WHAT RELATIONSHIP?

Business success relies upon implicit trust and a determination to share in a common purpose.

**Knowing that it is in our best interests
to succeed.**

The participants seek to understand each other's needs and – where there is a difference – negotiate to resolve the areas of conflict that prevent them from achieving the best result. The reconciliation of interests through negotiation calls for the practice of a high degree of interpersonal skill and a thorough understanding of the subject matter.

We suggest that the best way to achieve a proper understanding lies in identifying and analysing the strategic areas of interest to each party. Managers should choose to invest their resources in areas where tangible progress can be made towards attaining corporate and personal objectives. How does such analysis fit into the selection process to determine the most appropriate relationship to match the business to be discussed? The simplest way to examine this question is to put it into a commercial context – a buying and selling one.

A buyer, for example, has to work out which supplies and services are critical to operational success, whereas a supplier needs to evaluate which customer accounts can best repay the investment in time and effort to retain and develop the business. The choices facing the buyer are illustrated in Figure 2.1 by a spectrum extending from the competitive – and strictly formal arm's length setting – to one where vision and synergy are shared in a complementary partnership.

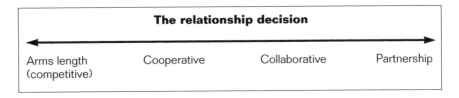

Figure 2.1 The Relationship Spectrum

Purchasing, like other business functions, cannot be considered in isolation and decisions have to be made as to what relationship is necessary or appropriate. The type of relationship, whether it be arm's length, cooperative, collaborative or partnership, governs the style and strategy of the negotiations within that relationship.

Two techniques that are helpful in deciding the most appropriate relationship are:

● supply positioning, as used by purchasing executives
   and
● supplier preferences, as used by supplier account executives.

The relationship and application of the two techniques require explanation, providing as they do a method of channelling management effort into the most productive areas of the business likely to yield competitive advantage.

SUPPLY POSITIONING

Supply positioning identifies, plots and segments purchases, relative to both their cost and the degree of risk they represent should supply be interrupted. The evaluation forms the basis for formulating a credible purchasing and negotiating strategy which embraces both the state of the supply market and the criticality – or other perceived classification – of the item within the plot of a market segmented into four quadrants (Figure 2.2).

It can be time-consuming to list all the goods and services that are purchased for an organization and then plot them into the four quadrants as in Figure 2.2, but if the purchasing activity is to be lifted into a strategic role

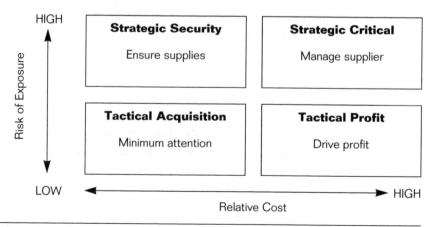

Figure 2.2 Supply positioning

within the organization and contribute significantly to profit, cash flow and corporate development, then it is essential.

SUPPLIER PREFERENCES

Supplier preferences identify, analyse and place the buyer's business in a segmented market made up to reflect the seller's vital interests (Figure 2.3). It enables the suppliers to evaluate the competitive position of their own firm in regard to other suppliers competing in the same market and to compare the attractiveness – or otherwise – of doing business when weighted against the relative value/cost equation. This is vital information to any supplier formulating a negotiating strategy.

MATCHING THE PARTIES

The best possible scenario is one where the buying and the selling parties share a common belief that each can realize their respective goals through a contractual relationship that supports this aim.

Given that the analysis by the buyer (Positioning, Figure 2.2) and the supplier (Preferencing, Figure 2.3) are conducted entirely independently of each other there is ample room for incorrect assumption and misunderstanding. It is timely to consider two aspects that may provide a clue to identifying the clear intention of the parties:

- **Power**   What is the power balance both from a person-to-person perspective and from the respective business-to-business angles?
- **Empathy**   Can we see and understand how and why the opposing party think and feel the way they do and what drives them?

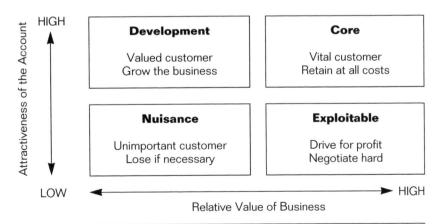

Figure 2.3   Supplier Preferences

It is our contention that the parties need to understand where the sources of power lie and from where pressure can be anticipated. This is a factor likely to affect the negotiation and the ultimate choice of relationship.

The use of empathy calls for good listening skills and self-control. We need, however, to ensure that the fine line between empathy and sympathy is not crossed.

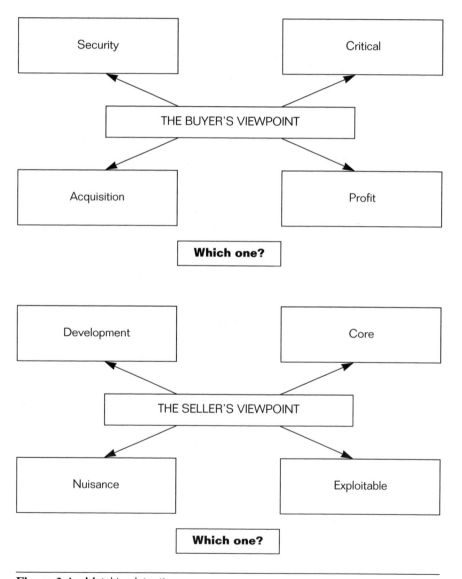

Figure 2.4 Matching Intentions

The importance of finding out at the earliest possible stage in negotiation how much the other party want the business cannot be overemphasised.

The answer to these and similar questions, which go to the heart of the relationship, need to be obtained at an early point in the contractual cycle. Care and attention has to be invested in a relationship to generate a genuine desire to reciprocate.

Irrespective of outcomes derived through the impersonal application of positional analysis, such decisions require validation through skilled dialogue to discover real intentions.

Any negotiation has, therefore, to take place on two interdependent levels if it is to succeed (Figure 2.5). Efforts will be concentrated in the personal dimension to alter mismatches of business grouping or categorization. The aim is to achieve a better fit of the segments (as in the examples of buyer and supplier analyses in Figures 2.2 and 2.3) towards an agreement of purpose which will ultimately underpin the relationship.

Whereas much general discussion has centred on the ideal of partnership, this should not be construed as a blanket endorsement in support of total commitment to that principle. Many business situations are resolved quite satisfactorily at differing levels of relationship. A partnership is by no means the only way to resolve business relationships.

Collaborative research ventures, as witnessed in the aerospace and motor industries, show that possibilities can be jointly studied without the necessity for concluding a strategic long-term relationship.

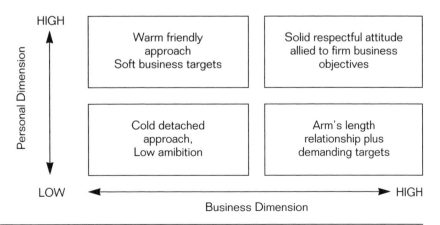

Figure 2.5   The personal and business dimensions

KEY POINTS

1. Clearly establish the nature of the difference between parties before deciding on the kind of relationship that needs to be fostered. Will the time frame matter?

2. Analyse the benefits and decide on the amount of effort needed to make the arrangement achieve what you want. How important is it to the business?

3. Think in terms of the other party. How attractive is the potential business to them? Do they need or want it? How does it fit into their portfolio? Clues to answers take effort to recognize. Signals in early negotiation will be detectable if you empathize and share the concerns of the other party.

4. Study the balance of power between interests and the respective parties. Power may flow from a position or appointment held, from the reputation of an organization or even from the latest development in the business picture. Expect leverage and conditioning from those used to exercising power – and be prepared to counter it.

5. Sales staff sell to customers but buyers deal with companies. Both deal with people as distinct from organizations but it is a point for reflection on how the different roles are perceived.

6. Negotiations – once started – proceed on two levels:

   - the personal
   - the business (or task)

   Despite the excellence and accuracy of analytical methods any changes to achieve a best fit (congruence) will largely rely on the efficient functioning of the person-to-person level.

7. The choice of relationships (as examined in Figure 2.1) influence the style that the parties are likely to adopt (more about this in Chapter 3) but the choices within the spectrum are essentially contractual by nature. How much reliance is placed on the written word when such trust would have been better invested in securing commitment on the personal level?

8. Negotiation is a two-way street. From our understanding of its nature (Chapter 1) there needs to be a genuine desire to create a climate in which pledges of trust can be

reciprocated. Shared warmth produces remarkable dividends once the parties are at ease and contributes to making the deal work.

9. Beware of the wolf in sheep's clothing! We have recently encountered buyers in the manufacturing sector with minds set upon adversarial intent whilst professing a belief in the benefit of partnership, thus offering every prospect of a bumpy ride. B. K. Pilling and L. Zhang, in their research, observed that 'power must be exercised judiciously. The use of coercive power in inter-firm relationships has been shown to weaken their cooperative nature' ('Cooperative exchange: reward and risks', *International Journal of Purchasing and Materials Management*, spring 1992).

What's next?

We will be looking at style.

Jot down the different styles of negotiation that your organization or enterprise employs to suit the circumstances.

---

3 WHICH STYLE?

When we observe the other party across the negotiating table we do our best to find out:

- how they are behaving
- the reasons for their behaviour
- if there are any inconsistencies between appearance and fact.

BEHAVIOURAL PATTERNS

It is understandable that we follow the mode of operating with which we are most comfortable. We almost certainly have a preferred style which we use without thinking. Observation of this style, as signalled by the outward show of our intentions, lends weight to predicting the most likely traits we and others can expect. Extensive studies have revealed common characteristics in behavioural patterns of people with the same occupation.

INFLUENCES ON STYLE – WHY PEOPLE BEHAVE AS THEY DO

We want to illustrate here the significant role played by the organization, ethics, ethos and personality in moulding negotiation style in a business context. The business negotiator has many pressures and influences that will affect their natural style (Figure 3.1).

STEREOTYPING

Just as in the acting profession so it is with negotiation. We associate leading performers with certain roles that established their reputation and this often leads to them being typecast in future roles.

We are also familiar with typical behavioural patterns which provide a rich vein for characterization, and so it is with people in general. We have a mental picture of how they will react and behave in certain circumstances. This picture is built up by our experience of them, and their behaviour is influenced by the factors shown in Figure 3.1. As negotiators it is important that we can recognize the stereotype and how they are typecast.

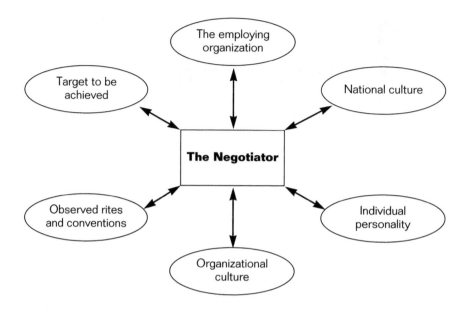

Figure 3.1   Influences on negotiation style

The successful outcome of a negotiation where the other party has been persuaded to move to a position closer to your own may well rely on the convic-
tion with which your case is delivered or its perception by the other party.
Can you succeed in appearing as a negotiator with personal warmth and yet
be cool and pragmatic in portraying that it will be hard to get your business
without substantial concession to your viewpoint?

Further extension of typecasting can be helpful in:

- establishing the type of person and anticipating how they are likely to
  behave
- predicting the effect of that style on the outcome of a prospective deal.

Recognition of the style displayed by the other party enables us to:

- feel more comfortable when a particular pattern of behaviour is being
  exhibited on the other side of the table
- keep the momentum from flagging when it appears to be petering out
- gain more information
- avoid or break an impending deadlocked situation
- better understand the effect of one's own tactics and appreciate those of
  the other party.

STYLE PROFILING QUESTIONNAIRE

How do you see yourself? . . .
Can you recognize your own negotiation profile?

Since we use negotiation – in different guises – in daily life, it would be invaluable to obtain an insight into the styles we most favour. You can do this by completing the following style profiling questionnaire adapted from A. M. Shelley's PMMS Consulting Group booklet (1989).

How to do the test
A negotiation situation will be described to you. There then follows a series of forced choice questions. You have three points to allocate between each pair of questions according to your preference. Here is an example. Imagine that you work on the fourth floor of an eight-floor office block. Your job requires you to change floors frequently. To do this you can either use the lift or the stairs. Your preference for using one or the other methods of changing floors (i.e. lift or stairs) will influence the way you allocate the three points.

When I change floors I use the lift	**L**	**0**
When I change floors I use the stairs	**S**	**3**

In this above example, you are saying that you always use the stairs. This is a strong preference.

When I change floors I use the lift	**L**	**1**
When I change floors I use the stairs	**S**	**2**

Here you are saying that you use the stairs most of the time. However, there are some occasions when you choose the lift.

When I change floors I use the lift	**L**	**1½**
When I change floors I use the stairs	**S**	**1½**

In this final example you are showing equal preference between the lift and the stairs.

Now go ahead and read the negotiation situation described. Then answer the paired questions that follow.

Scenario
You are the area manager responsible for letting the 'digital relay unit' contract. These units and related maintenance are hired from a company that you have been dealing with for some time. This company uses good equipment. The service quality over the past year has been good but not excellent. You currently hire seven units of the same specification. Due to business expansion, your forthcoming requirements will increase to nine units.

Bearing in mind the increase in volume, you are looking for a reduction in the unit price over what you paid this year. However, you would settle for a deal that required the same unit price as this year. Your boss would not complain if you could hold the increase to 5 per cent.

The sales manager, with whom you have struck up a good business relationship, has called to see you, to discuss next year's contract.

After the pleasantries you explain your need for two additional units. The sales manager thinks for a moment and then suggests a deal that will put you on the same unit price as you paid last year.

How do you respond?

The questionnaire provides fifteen pairs of responses. Allocate three points (no more, no less), between each of the pairs. Do this as in the example of the use of the stairs or lift.

Don't think too much! It is your immediate reaction that is important.

Style Profiling Questionnaire

1.	Accept the offer.	**A**
	Explain that you were looking for a 10 per cent reduction and ask to be met halfway, i.e. a 5 per cent reduction in price.	**C**
2.	Explain that you should also be looking elsewhere as a matter of company policy.	**T**
	Stress the 29 per cent increase in business you have to offer and the fact that the basic cost of equipment has fallen due to improvements in technology.	**L**
3.	Suggest improved payment terms and a longer contract period in exchange for a better offer.	**B**
	Show appreciation for the offer that has been made and mention the 'bad time' users have given you over servicing.	**E**
4.	Accept the offer.	**A**
	Stress the 29 per cent increase in business you have to offer and the fact that the basic cost of equipment has fallen due to improvements in technology.	**L**
5.	Suggest improved payment terms and a longer contract period in exchange for a better offer.	**B**
	Explain that you were looking for a 10 per cent reduction and ask to be met halfway, i.e. a 5 per cent reduction in price.	**C**
6.	Explain that you should also be looking elsewhere as a matter of company policy.	**T**
	Show appreciation for the offer that has been made and mention the 'bad time' users have given you over servicing.	**E**
7.	Explain that you were looking for a 10 per cent reduction and ask to be met halfway, i.e. a 5 per cent reduction in price.	**C**
	Stress the 29 per cent increase in business you have to offer and the fact that the basic cost of equipment has fallen due to improvements in technology.	**L**

8. Explain that you should also be looking elsewhere as a matter of company policy.	**T**
Accept the offer.	**A**
9. Suggest improved payment terms and a longer contract period in exchange for a better offer.	**B**
Stress the 29 per cent increase in business you have to offer and the fact that the basic cost of equipment has fallen due to improvements in technology.	**L**
10. Explain that you were looking for a 10 per cent reduction and ask to be met halfway, i.e. a 5 per cent reduction in price.	**C**
Show appreciation for the offer that has been made and mention the 'bad time' users have given you over servicing.	**E**
11. Suggest improved payment terms and a longer contract period in exchange for a better offer.	**B**
Accept the offer.	**A**
12. Stress the 29 per cent increase in business you have to offer and the fact that the basic cost of equipment has fallen due to improvement in technology.	**L**
Show appreciation for the offer that has been made and mention the 'bad time' users have given you over servicing.	**E**
13. Suggest improved payment terms and a longer contract period in exchange for a better offer.	**B**
Explain that you should also be looking elsewhere as a matter of company policy.	**T**
14. Explain that you should also be looking elsewhere as a matter of company policy.	**T**
Explain you were looking for a 10 per cent reduction, and ask to be met halfway, i.e. a 5 per cent reduction in price.	**C**
15. Accept the offer.	**A**
Show appreciation for the offer that has been made and mention the 'bad time' users have given you over servicing.	**E**

Now complete the results table on the next page

RESULTS

	Score
Number of points against A	
Number of points against C	
Number of points against B	
Number of points against T	
Number of points against L	
Number of points against E	
Total	45

Your negotiation profile

Shade in the squares below according to your score.

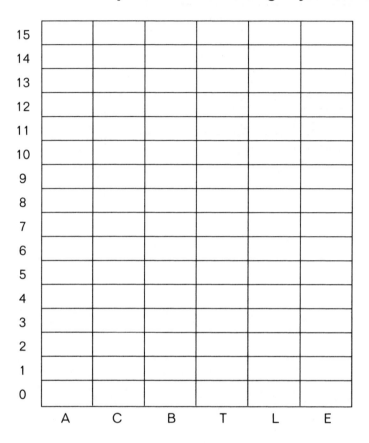

How did you fare?

Analysis of results

It is necessary to explain what the six letters mean at the bottom of the columns and the preferred scores. These scores and the comments made are taken from the results of many hundreds of questionnaires completed by PMMS delegates on training courses.

Column A – Acceptance

This column plots the number of times that you choose to accept the status quo and not negotiate. Any score at all in this column is weak. We would prefer that your score here is zero and that you show a greater desire to negotiate in order to improve your position. Everything is negotiable.

Column C – Compromise

This column represents the desire to seek the middle ground between your-self and the other party. By itself this is not a negative behaviour but it can be symptomatic of a lack of desire to push the negotiation boundaries to the limit and extract the maximum value from the deal. It is certainly better than not negotiating at all but it is not rigorous enough as a standard procedure. It is an easy option.

You should be looking for a low score here. Certainly not more than 4.

Column B – Bargaining

Bargaining is a method of extracting value from a deal by the exchange of various items ('variables') that each party values. Bargaining is a very worth-while activity but it does require that a person have something on offer to exchange. A score of between 6 and 8 is fine but not really more. There are more effective methods to put into practice.

Column T – Threat

The use of veiled or discreet threat can be a very powerful tool and should be part of every negotiator's portfolio. When used sensitively it can add a great deal of personal value to the deal and requires that you make no moves yourself. This is the first of the 'one-way' movers. These are approaches that can be employed to extract concessions from the other party that do not require any movement from yourself. Threat can be an antagonistic method and therefore should be used carefully.

A score of around 8 or 9 is appropriate – but not more.

Column L - Logic

The use of logic is a very common method of persuading the other party to make a concession. Logical reasoning is perhaps the tool in the box that is most regularly used in business negotiations. It requires the preparation of statistics and evidence so that one party can prove to the other that it is they who must make the concession. Certainly its correct use is to be recommended but it should not be used to the exclusion of other techniques. A score of around 11 or 12 would be appropriate.

Column E - Emotion
Emotion is one method of persuasion that is both 'free' and powerful. The ability to make the other party wish to move through goodwill or any other method concerning how they feel is the first and most potent method that should be employed by a trained negotiator.

A score of 12 plus is recommended here. It is the method that negotiators should seek to develop most effectively.

CONCLUSION

It is not our intention here to look at a supposed 'right' answer. We offer preferences but these can be revised in the light of many other factors. Both this workbook and *It's a Deal* (see Acknowledgements, p. viii) look extensively at these persuaders and any serious negotiator should be able to tune their style to make it both flexible and more effective.

Any profile reflects:

- individual personality
- the 'stamp' or style of the organization or that associated with that sector of employers
- culture or nationality.

This profiling would reveal differences between cultures, even within the UK. It can be a useful tool when preparing to negotiate with other nationalities.

As an example, the French share some, or all, of the following behavioural traits:

- proud
- nationalistic – fiercely patriotic
- love of their language
- reverence for the intellectual
- class-structured
- love of debate.

They are well known for exercising both emotion and power.

Any basic pre-planning would need to take account of such stereotyping and devise appropriate countermeasures if the behaviours are encountered when face-to-face negotiations commence.

KEY POINTS

1. Style is the outward manner in which people act.
2. It is an amalgam of influences shaped by:

   - individual personality
   - the ethos of the workplace
   - ethnic characteristics.

3. The skilled negotiator selects an approach to persuade the other party, and matches the style to fit – even if it is not their personal style.
4. Many people find a style that works for them and they stay with it, making them both predictable and vulnerable on that account.
5. The experienced negotiator is capable of continuing a warm relationship whilst being strong and firm in pursuing objectives.
6. Classifying people by their traditional traits into groups can be a useful learning exercise. However, the skilled negotiator can assume behavioural characteristics to match an out of character situation. Beware of investing too much trust in such classical stereotyping.
7. Practise using a style that is opposite to your natural inclination. Actors learn their lines and have to believe in the role they assume – so can you.
8. Achieve an understanding of the other party's intentions and beliefs at the earliest opportunity. To do this listen carefully and empathize with their situation and feelings as they see it.

What's Next?

You now have had an insight into:

● the nature of negotiation
● the necessity to consider the choice of relationship and the influence of style.

We can now proceed to look at the first of 20 steps in the process of developing a more effective personal style.

We have devised this workbook to progress you through 20 steps but we must emphasize that a flexible approach must be made to all negotiations. If you remain rigid you will become predictable.

Consider each Step as a tool or set of tools for your negotiating toolbox, to bring out and use when necessary. We do not intend that you follow rigidly from Step 1 through to Step 20 although some Steps do naturally flow from others. For instance, Objective Setting and Planning have to be early Steps but this does not exclude them from later stages of a negotiation when objectives may need to be reset or set for a different aspect of the negotiation. You must be prepared to use the tools, such as Questioning (Step 8) or Listening (Step 9) at any stage of negotiation.

PART 2

PRACTICAL NEGOTIATION

4 OBJECTIVE SETTING AND PLANNING

Successful negotiation requires a clear understanding of what is required and how this should be achieved. Before you enter the negotiation arena ensure that you have taken into account all the important issues.

A negotiation is not a casual conversation. It is an intensely personal activity which can exercise a wide range of emotions and often a large amount of calculation with a measured set of movements. You fail to prepare for this at your peril. You leave yourself vulnerable and could be easily exploited. This chapter seeks to start you off properly and thoroughly prepared. Follow this process and you will have a strong platform on which to build.

Step 1 *Why are we here?*

There are many definitions and techniques for drafting aims and objectives and looking for the means to achieve them. What is important from the start is one thing only – how to get the best deal. That's it, pure and simple. You can be negotiating a million-pound deal for your organization or trying to get a discount on your family holiday. The principle remains the same.

BUILDING A RELATIONSHIP

There is one question that should be asked first: 'Will I be seeing this person again?' This is a key point. There is a world of difference between the one-off negotiation (i.e. selling your house) where you will never see the other party again and the routine commercial negotiation where you have to regularly do business with the other party. This was clearly seen in the examples in Chapter 2.

Once you have resolved this question of relationships you can then progress. You can't move on until this question has been answered for one very important reason – as we have stated before, negotiation is an essentially personal activity and you have to define your relationship with the other party now and for the future before you can commence.

It must not be forgotten that even in the toughest of negotiations the power of an individual's feelings is paramount. There is no value in driving a great deal if it causes resentment and a desire for revenge that will sour business and could cost you more in the future than you could have saved in the short term. Conversely, if you are aware that the other party is going for broke in a one-off negotiation you can be properly prepared.

Most often it pays to make the other party feel warm towards you.

It is basic human nature that we feel more generous towards those people whom we like most. This makes even more sense if you see people regularly. However, if you will never see them again a much more aggressive approach could be an option.

Many will have heard of the double-glazing salespeople who can do a special deal 'just for you' and will pile favour on to favour in order to manipulate you into signing quickly. For them there is no second meeting and they will do whatever they can to work the deal in the short term.

WIN/PERCEIVED WIN

Your objective should always be to achieve a fine result for yourself and a feeling on the other side that they didn't do too badly either. This is the difference between Win/Win negotiation and what this book advocates, that is Win (by us)/Perceived win (by the other party). You think you've won but you'll manage the situation to ensure that the other party feel good about the deal and will be happy to return.

This is why expert negotiators never appear triumphant at the end of a negotiation and leave the other party feeling OK (maybe by having given them a small concession just as the agreement is about to be made). Such an approach should become an integral part of the planning process.

STEP 1   KEY POINTS

1. Identify the nature of the relationship that you have with the other party.
2. Don't try to win at all costs if you have a business relationship to manage for the future.
3. Remember that the other side is human too – they have feelings.

4. Why be hated when you can be liked.
5. Negotiation is a process of moving the other party.
6. Prepare yourself for the likely behaviour of the other party in the negotiation. Don't be taken by surprise.

Negotiation Scripts

Which of the following are useful and positive? Which should be avoided? Suggest reasons why and then compare your ideas with ours.

1. You'll have to do better than that, Mr Jones, I just can't afford it.

2. If you can't give me 20 per cent, Chris, I'm going to have to look elsewhere.

3. I've only got a budget for £100,000. You'll have to come down.

4. Come on, Steve, I'm sure there's some leeway in your price.

5. Look, Joanne, we managed to sort this out last time. I'm sure you can do something.

6. How much! Now come on, Mr Roberts, surely you don't expect me to pay as much as that this year.

OUR VIEW

1. This example is fine. It costs you nothing to say this and may well persuade the other party to consider moving.
2. This is poor. It puts down a marker, i.e. 20 per cent, which could limit your possibilities later. It may also be interpreted as a crude threat.
3. You've given away your budget. There are many issues in your planning that you need to keep to yourself. You should never reveal such information without careful thought.
4. There's nothing wrong here. You've used the other party's name which keeps it personal and potentially warm.
5. More names here. Remember that it costs nothing to ask. Keep it warm and friendly but be demanding.
6. Good use of emotion. You may not be a great actor but if you can do it in a style that suits you it could be effective. Remember, don't go over the top, it could damage your credibility.

Tactics and Counterplays

You need to be aware of the tricks of the trade. Use them at your discretion but above all be aware of when they are being used on you!

- **Personal friend**
  As a buyer be aware of sellers who are too friendly. They may not really mean it! This does not mean that you should never try to build a good relationship. Remember feelings can work on both sides of the deal.

- **Guilty party**
  Don't feel guilty if the other party tries to play the sympathy card. That's exactly what they want to happen.

- **Building trust**
  Make a real attempt to build a personal relationship with the other party. Always take the view that you negotiate with people rather than companies or organizations. Don't forget, though, that trust takes a long time to build.

- **Mr Nasty**
  If the other side act icy it may be because they are trying to make you feel uncomfortable. Equally it could indicate that they are in a weak position. Be sensitive to their behaviour and check it out. Try to understand why they are behaving in this way.

Exercises

We all know exercises are important. They keep you fit and ready to negotiate. Think of real examples and try to relate our theory back to your own experience.

1. Write down the three most important people or organizations with which you deal and find two words to describe the relationship you have with them.

2. Which supplier or customer do you dislike most? Which do you like most? How are your negotiations different with each one?

Negotiation Dilemmas

Here is an opportunity to test your knowledge against a set of difficult scenarios. What would you do in these situations? You can read our ideas after you have written your own.

Dilemma 1

Your house is on the market. After a quiet period with no potential buyers, a couple finally agree to view the property. After inspecting the whole house they look at you and say, 'It's not much of a house and we'd have to spend a lot of money on redecoration but we might be able to do a deal if you come down £10 000.' What are your choices?

OUR VIEW

The buyers have taken an aggressive tone but long-term relationships will not be important as this is obviously a one-off negotiation. The fact that they have made you an offer shows interest and represents good news. You must not be put off by the prickly tone. This could be just a ploy.

The buyers are making you feel uncomfortable and have put in a bid £10,000 below the asking price. Although you have had your house on the market for some time you should not be too eager here, for it could be that they are more desperate than you.

Some questioning would not go amiss!

You need to check out the buyers' situation. Assuming that you are prepared to make a small move on the price you could begin with 'We might be able to offer a small discount if you could move quickly. Are you in a chain?' This will help you gather information about their personal circumstances.

You could counter their comments about the decoration with use of emotion. 'It's a shame you don't like the decoration. It was something we took a lot of care about. Well, everyone has their own taste. How would you change it?' Now you can get them to start talking about 'how' they would change it rather than 'if' they buy the house. Try to replace 'if' with 'when'.

You know the price range in your area. £10 000 is their starting point. What is your first offer? You might offer a discount if they can offer you something: a fast move, payment for the carpets or curtains, etc. You should have your variables ready and try to trade them, but first go for one-way movement.

You can try a little threat. 'You're the third couple this morning', conditions them to think that the house is popular and that you will not accept a low offer. You also have the fall back of blaming the bank or building society for your not being able to accept their offer.

'We might be able to entertain a small discount', could start the ball rolling. Be prepared for their answer because they may well say, 'how much can you accept, then?' You're going to have to put down a marker at this stage. Remember to start low. £500 is a good starting point and will not damage your credibility. You want them to be thinking in *hundreds*, not *thousands* for the discount.

You may decide to move slowly towards them and make the deal. You may have to walk away. Whatever you do, don't be put off with a 'take it or leave it' approach (the answer is to leave it) and remember that the deal doesn't have to be done on the spot. They can always come back.

Negotiation Dilemmas

Here is an opportunity to test your knowledge against a set of difficult scenarios. What would you do in these situations? You can read our ideas after you have written your own.

Dilemma 2

Your regular sales agent visits you and tells you that he has just been given a final written warning because of his poor performance. He then tells you that if you can give him a double order he will be able to keep his job, otherwise he'll be fired. What is your reply?

OUR VIEW

This is your regular salesperson so you can assume that you know them well. You will have to know for yourself whether this is the truth or a ploy and your decision should be made accordingly.

Most people would see this as a tactic and a very crude one and would wish to counter it. There are various ways in which you can retaliate:

1. Try emotion yourself. You could tell them that business is also bad for you and that if you gave them a double order it could cost *you* your job.
2. You could call their bluff and burst out laughing. This is harsh and could well damage the relationship.
3. You could refuse and see if they return, and with what story.
4. You could offer the potential of a double order if they give you a good discount. Once you have received the discount you could then try to backtrack on the volume, but make sure that you have the capacity to store the extra volume and will use it.
5. Offer a small volume increase (for a big discount) as a gesture of goodwill.

Any of these five approaches could work but the way forward here is to try to exploit the situation to your own benefit. If it is genuine you could still try to turn it to your advantage. If it is just a ploy you can use it to explore the opportunities for volume discounts.

You could merely tell the other party not to use such a foolish tactic but this could cost you money in the long run. An expert negotiator tries to exploit the opportunity for a way forward in the deal rather than merely making a cold, tough statement which earns nothing.

Just Before you Finish

We finish each step with an opportunity for you to revisit key learning points with emphasis on what you are now going to try to do differently as a result. You should spend some time writing down these ideas and make a real commitment to action. There is space for three things to try to do. You should find at least one item for each step if you wish to get maximum value from the book.

1.

2.

3.

Step 2   What do we want to pay?

HOW MUCH BY WHEN?

It should be self-evident to every negotiator that it is better to enter into a business negotiation with a clear idea of the desired end result. This may, however, be a little more complex than first thoughts suggest.

Obviously the objectives should be stretching. If they are too easily obtained then you will be accused of not being rigorous enough. You must also ensure that you do not enter into a negotiation with a do-or-die target. If you have only one target and you achieve it very early you might stop trying at that stage and settle for second best. Your targets should be framed around expressions like 'as much as I can get' rather than '8 per cent'.

The plan here is to have a range of objectives, moving from the 'walk away' to the 'wow!' (Figure 4.1).

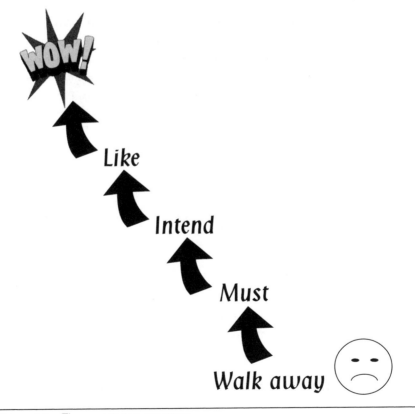

Figure 4.1   The negotiation spectrum

From a commercial buyer's perspective in a negotiation 'wow!' means free and 'walk away' means too expensive. The seller will have different aims: 'wow!' may mean full list price and 'walk away' may mean a certain maximum discount figure. Whatever your role in a negotiation it is at these two ends of the spectrum that planning is seen at its most important.

You should keep moving towards a golden scenario whereby you can achieve much more than you expected. Obviously you can damage your credibility if you constantly push towards the foolishly unobtainable but there may be circumstances about which you are unaware and which could be massively to your advantage. Never be the victim of your low ambitions and make sure that you test every assumption to the full.

'I'D LIKE IT FREE, PLEASE'

More is left on the table at the end of a commercial negotiation because of low expectations and lack of drive than for any other reason. As the adage says, 'If you don't ask, you don't get.'

As a buyer, why shouldn't you get it free? Perhaps not all of it but the first trial run, or a token sample, perhaps. Obviously you must not damage your professional credibility but if your answer to Step 1 is that you'll never be seeing this person again why not go for broke if it is morally and professionally acceptable.

If you are thinking from a buyer's perspective then **put yourself in the other person's shoes**. A commercial seller may wish to extend the sale to another department or obtain a reference to another potential client in the same organization.

It is important to maintain the highest credible aspirations and sustain the impetus towards achieving them.

'NOT TODAY, THANK YOU'

At the other end of the spectrum you must also have a position beyond which you cannot go. In domestic purchases we are all aware of the 'bank won't allow me' principle. Most of us would like to drive a Ferrari, if only . . .

If the other party knows that you cannot walk away then you are likely to be exploited.

In a commercial environment a monopoly situation often exists. They may need you and you cannot do without them. This requires special treatment but you must always let the other party know that there is a line beyond which you cannot move or if you are forced to move there will be serious negative consequences for them, if not now then certainly later.

THE NEGOTIATION ARENA

Between your two extreme positions you will have space in which you have freedom to move when the negotiating process begins. What you are seeking is similar space from the other party so that you both have an arena in which the performance can take place.

If there is no overlap in your prices and terms and conditions then there can be no deal. If your 'walk away' is so different from the other party's 'wow!' then you will not have an arena and you may both have to do business elsewhere. The negotiation arena is illustrated in Figure 4.2.

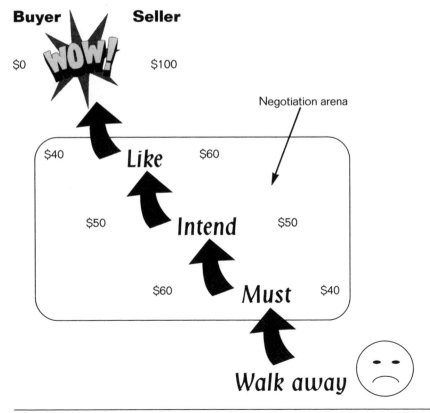

Figure 4.2 The negotiation arena

STEP 2 KEY POINTS

1. Always maintain a **range** of objectives.
2. **Aim high** and be persistent.
3. Be prepared to **walk away** when necessary or at least try to persuade the other party that you will.
4. If you're in a monopoly situation then emphasize the adverse consequences of their 'bad' behaviour if you believe that they are abusing their position.

Negotiation Scripts

Which of the following scripts are useful and positive? Which should be avoided? Suggest reasons why and then compare your ideas with ours.

1. I'm going to need the first batch free as a test run.

2. If you install it free, I'll be able to recommend you to my friends.

3. If that's your final offer I'm afraid we may have to call it a day.

4. I just can't afford it. Perhaps you could come back when prices have stabilized.

5. If you charge that much this year I'm going to have to reduce my order.

6. It's a lovely product but I just can't afford it.

OUR VIEW

1. Remember to aim high and ask. You'll have more success if you can keep the tone warm as you say it. Don't be antagonistic.
2. Excellent trade off. You do something for me (worth a lot to me) and I'll do something for you (at no great expense to me).
3. Don't say this unless you really mean it otherwise your credibility could suffer. When you hear this, test it out and see if they do really mean it. Remember there can be only one final offer or similar threat.
4. Using emotion to try to get a price reduction. You would love to buy it if only they could help. Try some emotion in return if this script is used on you.
5. This is clear threat so use it skilfully. They may call your bluff or it may give you some movement. When used on you, look for other issues to discuss besides volume and price.
6. The classic use of emotion to trump logic. A powerful technique. When used on you reply 'That's a shame' and see what response it elicits.

Tactics and Counterplays

You need to be aware of the tricks of the trade. Use them at your discretion but above all be aware of when they are being used on you!

- **Aim for the stars**
  Don't be put off if the other side's opening offer looks too high. They may have given you their 'wow!' They'll come down. It's common practice to aim high at first.

- **First is not best**
  Never accept the first offer. It is bound to be way above the 'must' position. It is almost a tradition that you do not accept, nor expect to have accepted, a first offer.

- **The final offer**
  Make sure it really is their final offer when they mention it. A good negotiator will never move on the 'final' offer but it's worth testing none the less. If they do move you have a powerful piece of information the next time they give you another 'final' offer.

- **Take it or leave it**
  Ask yourself if they really are prepared to walk away from this deal at this point. Is it real? You don't have to believe it just because they said so. Test it to see if they're serious. When in doubt it is better to leave it. You can always come back later.

Exercises

We all know exercises are important. They keep you fit and ready to negotiate. Think of real examples and try to relate our theory back to your own experience.

1. Think of the deals that you have done recently. Write down two ways in which you could have saved some money or added extra value to the deal.

2. List three ways in which you could get something free in a negotiation without damaging your credibility.

Negotiation Dilemmas

Here is an opportunity to test your knowledge against a set of difficult scenarios. What would you do in these situations? You can read our ideas after you have written your own.

Dilemma 3

You do your preparation for the negotiation and the process begins. After a short period the other side make an offer far in excess of your 'wow!' What is your response?

OUR VIEW

If your preparation was done properly you may have been truly fortunate here. What you might ask at this stage is whether your preparation wasn't a little skimpy and your 'wow!' wasn't set high enough.

It may be, though, that your homework was correct and the other party have made a palpable error. In this case you should refrain from doing a lasting deal until you have checked the figures very carefully. It may also be that the other side are experiencing business problems which have caused them to put together a desperate (and maybe untenable) deal.

None the less you have been pleasantly surprised and need to react. What you must *not* do here is to accept the offer. It is a well-known tenet of negotiating that you never accept the first offer, so you can reasonably assume that the other party still have plenty left to offer.

Using the 'thank and bank' principle you should obtain ownership of the offer by thanking them for it. At the same time you should try to warm up the other party by telling them that this is certainly a step in the right direction and you feel that good progress is being made. You must also make it very clear that they still have some way to go before the offer can be finally accepted.

A choice you need to make is whether to tell them that they still have a 'long way' to go or whether 'just a little more' is preferable. Both have their advantages and depend largely on your own personal style.

You may have to offer them something in return for further movement if you feel that the opportunities for one-way movement have been exhausted, but your planning should have taken care of that.

The key points of this dilemma are to aim high, be cautious and be flexible in achieving as much as you can get rather than aiming at any particular number.

Negotiation Dilemmas

Here is an opportunity to test your knowledge against a set of difficult scenarios. What would you do in these situations? You can read our ideas after you have written your own.

Dilemma 4

You have just started the negotiation when the other party puts an offer on the table and tells you 'Take it or leave it.' What is your response?

OUR VIEW

You are the recipient of a heavy threat and you need to respond to it skilfully. You need to look at the options. If you 'take it' you have given in to the other party and your credibility will have been reduced. The other party will know that you can always be threatened again with the likelihood that you will give way. If you 'leave it' what are the possible outcomes? First, the other negotiators may take you at your word, pack their bags and leave. This means that both you and they have lost the chance to do business. This may be acceptable at the end of the negotiation when you know you have reached a 'walk away' position. This is most unlikely at the start of the negotiation.

It can be readily assumed that a tactic such as this at the beginning of a negotiation is the sign of a less skilful player. This is a crude attempt at one-way movement and highly unlikely to succeed. Ask yourself whether the other side actually expect you to give in. No expert negotiator would be so heavy-handed so early on.

Your only realistic response here is to 'leave it' but this does not mean that you need necessarily walk out. You need to find the right tone.

The best suggestion is to reply with something that suggests that there are other options available. The reply 'I'm sure we can sort this out without resorting to such drastic measures' may prove useful. You might try to bounce the threat back. 'I hope that you are not going to make me walk away here. I think we can sort something out' is assertive and shows that you are prepared to fight your corner if necessary.

Heavy-handed threats are more often doomed to failure than to success. Don't threaten unless you are prepared to carry it through.

Just Before you Finish

List up to three things that you intend to do differently as a result of this step.

1.

2.

3.

Step 3   Pricing the variables

Now that you have a range of figures in mind to cover the major issues it is time to look at the variables in the negotiation.

If this is a new area of operation for you then imagine the purchase of a car. The price on the windscreen is only one of the considerations (variables) in terms of the cost of purchasing the vehicle. We need to look at the finance, warranty, stereo, extras, etc. All of these need to be included in the deal and each of these separate variables has to be costed with a range for each one.

This can be a time-consuming exercise but if you don't know the value of each variable it is difficult to be clear about the negotiation when the other party start to put their value on it.

Once you have begun this process it is important that you also seek to place a value on the variable from the other party's viewpoint. Once you know how much a dealer has to pay the manufacturer for metallic paintwork, for example, you have a better idea how high and low the dealer may go when this variable is added to the deal.

You will notice that both sides to a deal may price the same variable differently. One company needing fast payment may be willing to pay in terms of discounts for cash on delivery. Money to them will have a value beyond the opportunity costs which the other party may calculate.

Most commercial deals hinge on price, contract length, payment and volume but there can be dozens more variables. Identify them and price them before you enter the negotiation room.

FOREVER FOR NOW

Remember when pricing variables that the business of negotiation is dynamic. Pricing and valuing variables can change to suit changing circumstances. You must see the value of a variable in the light of changing information. This shows more than ever the importance of useful, up-to-date, market information.

Constantly reassess your position and your objectives in the light of new information.

YOUR BEST PRICE

You should not be so naïve that you believe that there is something that represents the 'best price' or 'lowest offer'. Any deal can change shape in an instant depending on the acquisition of new information. It is, therefore, not unreasonable to believe that there can be dozens of 'lowest prices' depending on the terms of the deal. Change the parameters of the deal and the 'best' deal available also changes.

PRICE AND COST

Experienced commercial operators know that the price on the tag, no matter how small or large, never represents the sole cost of purchasing or owning the product. Always differentiate between price and cost and don't focus too fully on price to the exclusion of other very valuable elements.

STEP 3   KEY POINTS

1. List every variable in the deal.
2. Organise a 'wow!' and a 'walk away' for each one.
3. It's the variables that make the difference between price and cost.
4. Value the variable from the other side's point of view, if possible.
5. Be flexible and ready to change values in the light of new information.

Negotiation Scripts

Which of the following scripts are useful and positive? Which should be avoided? Suggest reasons why and then compare your ideas with ours.

Imagine you are buying or selling a car . . .

1. Tell me about payment terms.

2. How much extra is a CD player?

3. If I could deliver it quicker how could you help me on price?

4. I'll buy it if you throw in a free service.

5. How important is the warranty to you?

6. I didn't realize it was that important to you. I'm going to have to reconsider this.

OUR VIEW

1. This is a straightforward request for information without committing yourself. Make sure that you ask in an appropriate way and another piece of information will be yours.
2. If you are buying a car and you can get a good deal on the CD player you will have added value to the deal without even mentioning price. Good use of variables here.
3. You have offered a variable and made it clear that you expect something in return. If you have done your homework then you will be able to value what is being offered and negotiate fully for its value.
4. You've said that you'll buy it if there's a free service. This means that you must be at the end of the deal and you are sure that you want it. Ensure that you do not commit yourself too quickly with statements like this.
5. It may be that you are not particularly worried about a warranty and you could trade it off against something more valuable. By asking this question you are gaining information from the other party without committing yourself.
6. This is a way of gaining time when you are under pressure. Without prejudicing your case you have time to consider what may be a new issue introduced into the negotiation.

Tactics and Counterplays

You need to be aware of the tricks of the trade. Use them at your discretion but above all be aware of when they are being used on you!

- **Free offers**
  Make sure you know the value of what the other side seem to be 'giving' away. It may be more expensive than you think. There are no free lunches.

- **Nickels and dimes**
  Remember that the price on the windscreen is not the cost of the car. Don't be seduced by low come-on prices with strings attached.

- **Standing room only**
  Don't be too hasty when the deal gets complicated. They may know the numbers better than you. Take a time out or book another meeting.

- **Where do we stand?**
  Summarize regularly to make sure that you're in control of what's going

on. Don't let the other party summarize. It's amazing how often they make mistakes in their favour that you may not notice.

- **The Colombo tactic (also known as 'one more thing')**
  You should be aware that it is quite common at the end of a negotiation for the other party to drop in one last variable. You are about to conclude when you hear, 'That does include free delivery, doesn't it?' They are daring you to walk away for what is comparatively a small issue. Be prepared for it and respond assertively.

Exercises

We all know exercises are important. They keep you fit and ready to negotiate. Think of real examples and try to relate our theory back to your own experience.

1. Think of the deals that you have done recently. List as many variables as you can that could gain you an advantage.

2. What could you exchange for almost nothing in a negotiation that could earn you a large reward?

Negotiation Dilemmas

Here is an opportunity to test your knowledge against a set of difficult scenarios. What would you do in these situations? You can read our ideas after you have written your own.

Dilemma 5

A car salesperson tells you that she can fit a £1000 stereo free of charge in the car you are negotiating for. You already have an excellent stereo that you want to install yourself. What is your response?

OUR VIEW

You are being offered something very valuable but something which at this stage of the negotiation you neither need nor want.

Under no circumstances offer any negatives here. If somebody wishes to give you something (that means anything at all) the only response that should pass your lips is 'thank you'. You may choose to flinch a little to show a small amount of disappointment if you think that their generosity is not particularly great.

So the first step is to 'thank and bank' the stereo. You now own it. At some stage later in the negotiation you can then trade it back in return for something that you do want. If alloy wheels or metallic paintwork are on your shopping list you can now say to the other party, 'Why don't we see if we can do a trade here. I'm prepared to forgo the stereo that you kindly offered me if you can include some alloy wheels in the deal.'

This should benefit both parties. The other side believe that they are getting good value for the swap. You are translating something you didn't require into something you do. It's a good move all round.

Far too many novice negotiators would not have accepted the stereo or would have taken it in a begrudging way. Both of these responses may deter the other party from giving more. The essence of negotiation is to persuade the other party to move unilaterally so they must be encouraged as much as possible and made to feel good about doing it.

The more the other side like you and the more gratitude you show, the more they are likely to want to give you. The reverse is also sadly true.

Negotiation Dilemmas

Here is an opportunity to test your knowledge against a set of difficult scenarios. What would you do in these situations? You can read our ideas after you have written your own.

Dilemma 6

You know that your supplier has more business than it can handle which is causing production, storage and delivery problems. How could you use this to your advantage?

OUR VIEW

You have managed to discover some useful strategic information about the other party. You can now use this to your benefit. You may also be able to use this to the other party's benefit too. There is no reason why you cannot both create some extra value in the deal by collaborating.

You need to judge how best to let the other side know about your knowledge. You could drip it into the conversation and slowly let them become aware that you are fully briefed. You could also score a point in one particular issue if it will give you some negotiation leverage.

Do not use the information to humiliate or shame the other negotiator or company personally. This will cause resentment and be counter-productive.

As the problems surface you can try to suggest solutions that will add value. Ensure that whatever you suggest is profitable to yourself. Be prepared to look and sound helpful and try to create an atmosphere of trust.

It would seem in this example that the other company has quite a pleasant problem. You may be able to help them with storage and examine delivery schedules. If business is this good you should between you be able to create opportunities for value.

You will have to divide this extra profit later between you but do not be afraid to show some helpfulness at this stage. Some hard negotiating will be required when you start to claim your share of what has been created.

Good negotiators always create extra value. They do not merely fight over the number of slices in the cake. One of their primary tasks is to grow the cake.

Just Before you Finish

List up to three things that you intend to do differently as a result of this step.

1.

2.

3.

Step 4   What do we want to know?

Once you have planned your targets and defined the parameters of the negotiation you need to gather information and start to examine what facts you can use to support your case and weaken the arguments of the other party.

Remember to research all aspects of the negotiation, both commercial and human. You need to explore those factors that will give you leverage and facilitate movement.

SWOT

A SWOT analysis will help here: what **strengths** do you have; what **weaknesses** can you expose in the other party; what **opportunities** exist for you and the other party both individually and jointly; and what **threats** exist that require attention.

Ideally all of these facts will be available and will prove a sound platform for the upcoming negotiation. More often these facts are not available and require an element of assumption and educated guesswork. This is when you can be at your most vulnerable.

CHECK AND THEN CHECK SOME MORE!

If you predicate a position built on assumption or perception then you are on very thin ice unless you can subsequently check these assumptions. It will soon become very clear, therefore, that one of the first stages of any negotiation is to check and validate the 'homework' that has been done in advance. A key task is to prepare a list of the questions that you will need to ask to verify your preparation.

WHAT IF?

There is one further element of planning that should concern you – the contingencies, the 'what-ifs' of the process. It is this type of planning that gives the necessary flexibility to the negotiation.

There is little point in formulating a powerful Plan A if the assumptions and facts on which it is based are faulty. The reaction of the other party will also affect the routeplan. Rigid overplanning is the enemy of the creative and flexible negotiator.

Make sure that you possess a variety of routes, plans and strategies based on every conceivable 'what-if' that you can devise. Time spent on this area of planning will never be wasted. Flexibility is key to success.

FACT vs. REALITY

You will have some perception of the relative balance of power between yourself and the other party. It is important to remember that the perception of who has the power and leverage can be very different from the actual position. You may believe that you need the deal rather more than the other party. You should not allow this to change your position. Experience may well prove that the other side is more desperate than you are.

It is important to try to examine the situation from both ends and under no circumstances allow the other party to be aware that you may be 'desperate'. Remember that desperate people generally pay desperate prices!

STEP 4   KEY POINTS

1. Concentrate particularly on your strengths and the other party's weaknesses. Research shows that all too often we tend to do the opposite. (1)
2. Check out all of the opportunities and threats (be creative).
3. Be aware of the assumptions you are making and check them as soon as you can.
4. Have a variety of approaches. Be flexible.
5. Be aware of the possible reactions to your questions and have contingencies ready.
6. Keep an open mind on your real position of power compared with the other party.

Negotiation Scripts

Which of the following scripts are useful and positive? Which should be avoided? Suggest reasons why and then compare your ideas with ours.

1. As you know, ours is the market leader in quality and technology.

2. I understand that you're having some sourcing problems from Korea.

3. That surprises me. What leads you to make such a comment?

4. Well, why don't we try a different approach. I've got another idea I've been working on.

5. This is not a particularly urgent matter. We are looking at a range of alternatives over the next few weeks.

OUR VIEW

1. You are positioning your product so that the other party will be conditioned to think positively about it and you are also implying that there will be a premium to pay for such a quality product.
2. You've done your homework on the other party. You need to choose the right moment to let them know that you may have an advantage over them. Play this card skilfully and make sure that you get a payback for using it.
3. Expressing 'surprise' costs you nothing and forces the other party to have to explain their thinking. You are driving the conversation with comments like these.
4. Using good collaborative language makes the other party feel that you are both working together on the project. Creating value is a key activity. You can always divide it later.
5. You are letting it be known that you have no urgency on this matter. This may be a smokescreen so if it is used on you explore the comment with some questions rather than take it at face value. This is a ploy to gain a perceived advantage: you need it more than I do.

Tactics and Counterplays

You need to be aware of the tricks of the trade. Use them at your discretion but above all be aware of when they are being used on you!

- **Poker face**
  When faced with a tough proposal use noncommittal language. The reaction 'interesting' is always a good stonewall reply.

- **On the backburner**
  Try to put a tough question from the other party 'on the backburner'. If you leave it until later the other party may have forgotten about it or you may have been given enough time to find an answer. Don't let this happen to you. If you have an important issue to discuss always place it high on the agenda and keep re-visiting it.

- **Casual under fire**
  Under no circumstances allow the other party to think that you are desperate. If you are fortunate to discover this of the other side raise your expectations accordingly. Be mindful of your language and try your best to manage the other party's perception of your position.

Exercises

We all know exercises are important. They keep you fit and ready to negotiate. Think of real examples and try to relate our theory back to your own experience.

1. Think of the two people with whom you have dealt recently. Write down what you think their greatest weaknesses are both personally and corporately.

2. What do you think that your negotiation opponents might regard as your personal or corporate strengths and weaknesses? Be honest.

Negotiation Dilemmas

Here is an opportunity to test your knowledge against a set of difficult scenarios. What would you do in these situations? You can read our ideas after you have written your own.

Dilemma 7

You go into the final stages of an important negotiation fully prepared. You ask your initial fact-finding questions and discover that the spreadsheets you have prepared include a fatal arithmetic error. Cancelling the meeting is not an option. How else might you react?

OUR VIEW

Everybody makes mistakes in negotiations. This one has been discovered before any damage has been done, despite it being at the end of a negotiation and corrective action should not prove difficult.

If your credibility would suffer if you admitted the problem ask yourself how much more it would suffer if you continued with your flawed calculations or tried to make do and then had your bluff called.

How, then, do you extricate yourself? This is best done openly and honestly. If the mistake can be rectified simply a recess may be appropriate. You may be able to call back to base and get something couriered or e-mailed across. If this is not possible and the information forms the crux of the discussion you may have to ask for an adjournment.

This would mean that the part of the discussion on which the calculations depended would have to carried over to the next meeting. It might, though, be possible to continue the meeting by discussing and negotiating other issues that are on the agenda.

A palpable error will always invalidate a negotiation. It is not best professional practice to capitalize on an error. The other side will nearly always spot it and it will cause resentment and distrust and a lot of wasted time.

Some measure of apology may be required.

When things go wrong the test of professionalism is how well you put them right. Admitting your errors and apologizing will allow you to retain as much credibility as possible. Don't blame anybody and don't offer any whinging excuses. Put your hands up and plead guilty.

The other party may try to use this as a lever to obtain concessions. Use emotion to counter them. 'Come on, we all make mistakes, don't we?' may help your cause. 'You're not going to take advantage of me just because I've made a small error, are you?' may be worth a try in the right circumstances. You may even be able to create some personal goodwill if you handle this with tact and a pleasant manner.

There are many well-known instances of incorrect calculations causing major problems. For example, the leading car manufacturer who accepted a 106 per cent increase on batteries only to discover many months later that the correct figure was 16 per cent.

Negotiation Dilemmas

Here is an opportunity to test your knowledge against a set of difficult scenarios. What would you do in these situations? You can read our ideas after you have written your own.

Dilemma 8

You enter into a negotiation knowing that the other party have major cash flow problems and are on the edge of potential bankruptcy. They are also offering a deal that seems too good to be true. You're sure that they could not afford to finance what they are promising. How do you react?

OUR VIEW

You have done your preparation and you know that the other party cannot possibly afford what they are offering. There is no point in trying to grab a good deal if the deal will not hold up in the future. What is needed here is some risk analysis.

The price is not the cost of any deal. One of the principal factors in calculating cost is risk. What is the risk in changing suppliers? How much cheaper will they have to be in order to justify taking the risk? Does the company have a long-term future? Are they headed towards bankruptcy?

So here you have to ask yourself 'Is this deal worth the risk?' You must then re-evaluate your parameters so that they take this new factor into account. It may be that the other party have lost so much credibility that you would not wish to trade with them under any circumstances.

Again, as in other examples, some openness and honesty is called for. You should explain that you find it difficult to understand how they are able to offer such a deal and that you require evidence and back up. Do so in a warm tone being 'happily surprised' by their prices. You should already have completed your cost analysis and asking here for a price breakdown may help your case.

The other party may become cold and hostile and accuse you of lacking trust but you must wade through these comments and continue.

If necessary you should show your evidence to prove your point. Use a helpful tone and do not in any way suggest that the other party are lying. You could, in fact, be incorrect and there may be issues that are unknown to you. That is why you should not antagonize the other party – you may be missing a great business opportunity.

In any negotiation there will be certain variables for which some parties will be prepared to pay more than the going rate. Fast payment will suit a company with a large overdraft. They may be prepared to pay handsomely for early money. This does not mean that they are unreliable or have terminal problems.

If you can discover the weaknesses of the other party in advance you can then exploit them. Remember, though, that they are doing the same to you. Be prepared.

Just Before you Finish

List up to three things that you intend to do differently as a result of this step.

1.

2.

3.

Step 5   Organizing the case

During this preparation phase of the negotiation process it soon becomes necessary to arrange the issues based on your research and planning. You should have a clear outline of the direction that you wish your case to take with an equally clear outline of what you expect from the other side.

What is important here is not to arrange numerous reasons why or why not something may be the case but to look at the key elements and start to base your ideas around them.

Facts are an important method of persuading the other party and the quality of your arguments rather than the quantity will prove vital. However, if you are going to base your case on facts, make sure you've got them right and don't take the chance of assuming that the other party won't check them.

THE OTHER PERSON'S SHOES

Look at the positions you have adopted and start to rehearse why people would wish to move in your direction and accordingly try to play devil's advocate and predict the potential counter-arguments of the other side.

Always spend as much time as possible trying to understand the case from the other party's viewpoint. What is their plan? How will they implement it? What constraints does their business put on them? You must address these issues.

Remember, good negotiators always put themselves in the other person's shoes.

Where is the pain for them and where is the pleasure? Your task is to convince them that dealing with you will minimize their pain and maximize their pleasure.

A pot can be half empty or half full. Seeing from the other person's position will help you to understand their perceptions as well as their facts and information.

ECONOMY SIZE
Is it large or small?
A minicar or a large packet of soap powder are both economy size – it's a question of perception.

DILUTION

Do not dilute the issues by having too many, the majority of which may not stand much interrogation. Stand by your guns and if you have just one or two outstanding issues develop them with evidence rather than merely trying to add to them.

Issues are not like bullets. More is not better. More issues will not necessarily add value to a case. Creating a long list can be self-defeating if the last items on the list are not worth much.

Assertively repeating your best point is always better than adding others. Remember that the other party will try to get you to dilute your position.

This principle will stand you in good stead in the heat of battle when you are requested to 'prove' your point or 'justify' your position.

STEP 5   KEY POINTS

1. Research your position carefully.
2. Check out your competitors and their products and ideas.
3. If you were on the other side, how would you develop the case against your position?
4. Quality rather than quantity is important for logical reasoning.
5. Make sure that your case is sound and has a sensible base.
6. Identify the weak areas in your position and be prepared.
7. But be careful. Research shows that we too readily concentrate on our weaknesses and forget our strengths.

Negotiation Scripts

Which of the following scripts are useful and positive? Which should be avoided? Suggest reasons why and then compare your ideas with ours.

1. Really, Sir Alan, there's only one point that needs to be made and that is . . .

2. I've got a real problem with what you're saying and I'm afraid I can't move on until we've addressed it.

3. Let me show you our research. I've had two people working on it full time since we met last.

4. That's a good point you've made but I think you'll find that there's more than one answer. Let me show you my figures.

OUR VIEW

1. Lots to like here. You've used the name to keep the case personal and you have assertively returned to the one point that is important to you. You are in control and the tone is positive.
2. These words depend entirely on tone. If they are said in a positive manner then it could be part of a robust but friendly debate. If the tone is hostile then these words could prove to be destructive. Beware, however, you have signalled movement.
3. You are clearly making the point that you believe your logic to be good and you're about to prove it. Get your logic in first.
4. You are using logic to refute their argument. Always interrupt as quickly as you can. You don't want them to 'prove' too much before you can 'disprove' it, or a trend of fighting and defend/attack spirals can start.

Tactics and Counterplays

You need to be aware of the tricks of the trade. Use them at your discretion but above all be aware of when they are being used on you!

- **Argument dilution**

  If you can't overcome their logic ask for as many extra reasons as you can. They will finally start to give you some weaker ones which may allow you back in the game. Don't let it happen to you. Keep referring back to your one or two best points.

- **Logic battles**

  Get your case in first. Be prepared to interrupt people who are in the process of telling you 'why not'. Immediately start to tell them 'why'. Always shoot first in any logic battle. The first logical reasoning is often the best.

- **Emotion trumps logic**

  When faced with an incontrovertible fact use an emotional response to counter it. Expressions such as: 'I just don't like it' or 'the deal just doesn't seem to appeal to me' often beat dozens of well-argued statements.

- **The joys of software**

  If you want to support your arguments or destroy the opposition take a laptop computer into the room and ask for a couple of minutes to run their proposal through your software. You can then tell them that the computer has rejected their arguments and that you are not allowed to change its parameters. Remember that they may have a computer too!

Exercises

We all know exercises are important. They keep you fit and ready to negotiate. Think of real examples and try to relate our theory back to your own experience.

1. If you could go into your next negotiation with only one argument concerning price reduction what would it be? How would you present it?

2. Who are your biggest competitors at the moment? What is their biggest advantage against you? What is their biggest weakness? How can you exploit this?

Negotiation Dilemmas

Here is an opportunity to test your knowledge against a set of difficult scenarios. What would you do in these situations? You can read our ideas after you have written your own.

Dilemma 9

You are looking for a price reduction but the other party produce a large amount of statistical evidence concerning rising raw material prices and wage inflation. How do you counter these arguments?

OUR VIEW

This is a comparatively simple situation. You are into logic and the tactics are straightforward.

If you know that 'proof' is likely to be a key issue make sure that you get yours in first. It may be that you have already lost the initiative here because you have allowed the other party to tell you 'why' before you have had the chance to tell them 'why not'.

It is a simple but effective rule that the person who fires first in a logic war has the advantage. Get your logic in first and let them 'pick' on your case.

If you have lost the advantage the route forward now is to use emotion. Emotion always beats logic but it has to be applied in a professionally appropriate way.

Your reply to comments concerning raw materials prices and inflation should be along the lines of 'I appreciate all of your arguments, but if I can't afford it, that's all there is to say.'

Let them justify their prices. You merely have to reply that your budget won't stretch to the new amount. You could then try a hint of threat with something like, 'I know you think you can justify your new prices but it would be a shame if it was this price rise that drove us to consider a fundamental new approach to your product.'

It may be possible to try to beat some of their logic with some of your own but you must be *well prepared* and ready to fight them on their own ground. They will have done all their homework and it will show if you have not.

You could try some argument dilution. Listen to their arguments and get them to put down as many of their reasons as possible. Your hope is that finally they will present one that is weak enough for you to attack.

Negotiation Dilemmas

Here is an opportunity to test your knowledge against a set of difficult scenarios. What would you do in these situations? You can read our ideas after you have written your own.

Dilemma 10

You have foolishly asked the other party to justify their price rise. They have taken the opportunity to speak for a solid five minutes with innumerable arguments and reasons. Your head is beginning to ache and the tide is flowing against you. What do you do?

OUR VIEW

This is a matter of control. You must intervene in an appropriate way to try to press the pause button.

The most successful way to intervene in a conversation is to use a behaviour label. This is a means of prefacing what you are going to say with a comment that prepares the other party. You should then match these words with the appropriate body language.

As you lean across the table with your arm out you utter the words 'I wonder if I could interrupt you for a moment and ask a question. Something you have just said really interests me.' You then ask a question followed by another. This puts you back in control.

You have used friendly non-aggressive words so there has been no hint of your saying 'shut up!' You have also used the intriguing words 'really interests' which is bound to make the other party more likely to want to hear what you want to say.

As you have leaned across the table with your arm out you look as if you mean business which adds weight to your words.

If you find that the other party insist on continuing and ignore your comments then you must persist with something like 'I really must interrupt, John, to ask my question. It is important to me.' If this does not succeed you should try yet again with 'John, I'm not able to listen any more, I'm afraid, without asking my question. What I'd like to know is . . . .' You then continue.

Behaviour labels are an excellent way of ensuring that your interruption or question always carries maximum effect.

Just Before you Finish

List up to three things that you intend to do differently as a result of this step.

1.

2.

3.

5 THE FIRST PHASES

Step 6   *When do we start?*

If you're thinking about when to start a negotiation it may already be too late. It may have started much earlier than you thought. Commercial negotiations start at the first meeting, receipt of correspondence or telephone call. It is never too early to begin in terms of conditioning the other party, shaping their expectations or creating a powerful first impression. The end of your next negotiation could be the beginning of the one after.

At the personal level the power of the first impression is well understood. 'Love at first sight' certainly makes the negotiation go more easily! Even before then the quality of the notepaper, advertising or just the efficiency of the administration creates the right sort of impression.

CONDITIONING

It must not be forgotten that a powerful impression shapes expectations. It should be your desire right from the outset to condition the other party that they are dealing with a serious professional and their expectations should be set accordingly. If you get it wrong then their aspirations may rise before you have even sat down at the table.

This applies to the way that you dress, the car that you drive and the demeanour that you bring to the table. All of these should be part of your plan. Ensure that you use every means to create a winning scenario. Here are some ideas. You can add your own to them:

- Ensure that your paperwork is faultless.
- Make your telephone contacts professional.
- Sow some seeds of ideas to shape expectations.
- Ensure that the negotiation room is well prepared.

You want the other party to come into the room with low expectancies and you should say or do nothing to jeopardize this.

SOME PRELIMINARY DIGGING

Most preparation hinges on what you are going to do when you get to the meeting. Expert negotiators have already dug the ground. Plan to send some preliminary documentation, some information material or anything that may help shape the perceptions or expectations of the other party in a direction favourable to you *prior* to the meeting..

STEP 6   KEY POINTS

1. It is never too early to start the negotiation.
2. Be aware of the power of first impression.
3. Manage all aspects of your behaviour and keep them positive.
4. Do your best to reduce the aspirations of the other party.
5. Keep emphasizing one or two key points prior to the meeting to sow some seeds in their minds.

Negotiation Scripts

Which of the following scripts are useful and positive? Which should be avoided? Suggest reasons why and then compare your ideas with ours.

1. Let me pass you over to my personal assistant. He handles all of my appointments.

2. Can I offer you a coffee? I've taken the trouble to ask the caterers to prepare a small buffet. We always do this for important customers.

3. I'm pleased you received our literature. We asked Saatchi and Saatchi to prepare it for us this year.

4. I can spare you ten minutes but I don't normally deal with the smaller accounts.

5. Margins are tight this year. We're certainly not expecting to suffer any price rises.

OUR VIEW

1. This is a piece of one-upmanship: 'So you're important enough to have a PA, eh?' 'So I'm not important enough to be dealt with by you.' This will impress some people and antagonize others. It's your choice.
2. Now you're an important customer. Flattery may get you somewhere. Say it sensibly and with some reasonableness and they may even believe it!
3. Again you're in the business of creating a good impression. These sort of comments have to be handled well otherwise they will clang badly and put people off.
4. This will definitely cause problems. It might do your ego good but if it is at the expense of a customer then it's a serious mistake.
5. Conditioning is always a good strategy. You are trying to ensure that your key messages have already been received before the first meeting or at least not long into it.

Tactics and Counterplays

You need to be aware of the tricks of the trade. Use them at your discretion but above all be aware of when they are being used on you!

- **Desperate Dan**
  Never look or sound too eager. It leads the other party to think that you need them rather more than they need you.

- **Timing is everything**
  Book appointments at five or ten minute sections of the diary. Meetings do not have to start on the hour or half hours.

- **God's right hand**
  Pay attention to where people sit in the room. Let them sit down first and then position yourself near to the decision maker. If you wish them to sit where you prefer you could try to use nameplates.

- **I'm busy but . . .**
  Remember that your diary is always full of important meetings. You might just be able to fit them in for a negotiation if you do a bit of juggling! Never have an empty diary (even if it is).

- **Dear John!**
  Never forget the power of a mail merge. Keep all mailshots personal.

- **Senior executive**

  If you have a junior sounding job title do not put it on your business card. Just your department will do. On the other hand if you are the boss let them know. Skilled negotiators are always happy to see the boss – once they agree who can stop them?

Exercises

We all know exercises are important. They keep you fit and ready to negotiate. Think of real examples and try to relate our theory back to your own experience.

1. Write down three important ways in which you could start to condition the other party before they have even come into the negotiation room.

2. How might you improve your image and try to influence the perception of the other party during that important first impression phase?

Negotiation Dilemmas

Here is an opportunity to test your knowledge against a set of difficult scenarios. What would you do in these situations? You can read our ideas after you have written your own.

Dilemma 11

You walk into a room and the other party are sat behind a large desk. They ask you to sit 10 feet away. How do you react?

OUR VIEW

You are the recipient here of an old-fashioned power play. You are being conditioned to the idea that the other party have power and authority and that you are at a disadvantage.

Good assertive behaviour demands that you make a comment that is professional and friendly. Comments such as 'Excuse me but I'm finding it difficult to concentrate with the light from the window right in my eyes. Do you think we could move?' are hardly likely to be refused.

You may wish to put up with the discomfort if you feel that there is a good reason for so doing and that it furthers your case. You must never suffer anything because of fear or embarrassment. In this particular case you should immediately seek to reorganize the room letting the other party know that you are unable to begin the negotiation.

You should ensure that the tone of the meeting remains warm throughout. You would not wish your comments here to jeopardize further opportunities in the negotiation. It may, however, be appropriate to return the tactic with one of your own: 'Nice office, Mr Smith, I had one like this last year before they promoted me.' If it sounds facetious don't bother but you should at least let the other party know that you are aware of the ploy.

Negotiation Dilemmas

Here is an opportunity to test your knowledge against a set of difficult scenarios. What would you do in these situations? You can read our ideas after you have written your own.

Dilemma 12

You usually meet the buyer when you visit your customer. This time you are shown straight into the Managing Director's office. How do you react?

OUR VIEW

Ask yourself why the buyer should suddenly give way to the MD. Something is going on and you should be wary.

It would be polite to ask why the arrangements have been changed. You should immediately greet the MD and encourage as warm an atmosphere as appropriateness will allow. This is an opportunity – grab it.

You should be a good listener at this stage and also make sure that any questions you have or doubts in your mind are fully explored before you embark on the negotiation.

If the MD is there to offer some form of threat you should acknowledge this inwardly. Circumstances have hardly changed merely because of a change in personnel. If they have changed you should check them out and react accordingly.

Obviously the other party see your negotiation as important. You should try to think what circumstances have arisen that could have prompted such a move. This may be a move in your favour if you can only discover the real reason. Prices and targets should automatically be adjusted upwards if you think that this is a sign of weakness by the other party.

The MD is a decision maker. You should ask yourself if this is a buying signal and whether you have the opportunity to close on the deal. The MD would not be there if there was no hope of a deal. Don't be overawed by position. You must be important for the MD to bother with you.

Good negotiators see only opportunities, never problems – here you have someone others can't overrule.

Just Before you Finish

List up to three things that you intend to do differently as a result of this step.

1.

2.

3.

Step 7 The opening round

WHERE AND WHEN

After considerable planning and thought it is now time to meet the other party. Of course you must, yourself, decide on where and when. Make sure that you place the meeting at the location best suited to yourself and least suited to the other party. If you are a buyer, for example, you should be aware that sales people routinely work away from home. Why not visit them? Remember, it's much easier to leave when you're in the other party's office.

If you do have the meeting at your office make sure that the room adds to the impression. If you are based in an open plan office borrow a room. Manage the location to provide the impression you require.

Consider also the timing. Very few sellers want to talk on a Friday afternoon. How many buyers would visit a supplier first thing Monday morning?

Be aware of your own body clock. If you're a lark have an early meeting and use your morning energy. If you're an owl don't be bleary eyed at an early meeting when you could be motoring in the afternoon.

'HELLO'

Now it's time to meet. Remembering what we know about first impressions we know how vital this stage is. Here's a checklist to remind you:

1. BE ON TIME – never late!
2. Good, firm handshake.
3. Maintain eye contact.
4. Smile.
5. Use the other person's name (make the meeting personal).
6. Exchange business cards and look at them respectfully.
7. Provide *good* refreshment.

You'll never get another chance to manage your relationship with other people as much as you can during this first meeting.

WHO AM I?

Now that you've met your visitor it's time to acknowledge them personally. Who is he or she? What's their role in the company? Did he or she have a good journey? Would they like a cup of coffee or tea?

When faced with a team of negotiators you should try to discover which of the group is the decision maker. Once you have this knowledge you can then direct your arguments accordingly. The obvious counterploy is to ensure that you do not reveal this to the other party. You can call yourself the 'project' team with joint responsibility.

In Chapter 2 we asked 'why be hated when you can be liked?' So this is the best way to start: slowly and with proper observation of the social niceties expected within the culture, which acknowledges your visitor as a valued guest, makes them feel warm towards you and starts the questioning process, whereby you can start checking your assumptions and validating your research.

THE POWER TO NEGOTIATE

One of your first tasks is to check that the person or team opposite has the power to negotiate and the authority to take decisions. You could be putting yourself to a great deal of inconvenience and time wasting if the other side have to report back and lack the required authority to make a decision on the spot. You could give a lot away and get nothing in return.

WHO'S NORMAL AROUND HERE?

When questioned most people from whatever walk of life will admit to being pretty 'normal'. That means a regular way of dressing, talking, behaving, having normal social, moral and political views, etc.

It goes without saying that people feel most at home when they are dealing with others who are 'normal' like them. This creates a state of rapport and allows people to relax and feel that they are dealing with someone whom they can trust. This is why people join clubs and societies and wear badges that identify them as 'normal' to fellow clubmates.

People prefer to deal with people like themselves – build empathy and rapport so they will see you as a 'like spirit'. The more the other party sees themselves when they look at you the easier they will find it to do business. An expert negotiator is, therefore, a social chameleon changing to suit each individual with whom they have to deal.

Obviously when this technique is used badly it looks artificial and manipulative but when used subtly the usual feeling is one of trust and understanding.

STEP 7   KEY POINTS

1. Play the game at the best venue and organize the kick-off time.
2. Manage the first meeting by creating a powerful personal first impression.
3. Get to know the other side. Know them as people not just opponents.
4. Keep the atmosphere warm and friendly for this first meeting.
5. Try to mirror the other party and create an atmosphere of trust.

Negotiation Scripts

Which of the following scripts are useful and positive? Which should be avoided? Suggest reasons why and then compare your ideas with ours.

1. Fine office you have here. Open plan certainly has its advantages!

2. That's a fine sun tan you've got. Did you have a good holiday?

3. I see you've got a new car. How do you like it?

4. I see you're in Rotary, Mr Williams. I'm in my local club.

OUR VIEW

1. This is a two-edged sword. It could be a compliment or it could be a sharp comment about not having a personal office. Be careful, it's not what you say but how it's taken that is important.
2. Why not make some small talk as long as both sides deem it appropriate. There's no need to get down to business straight away. Try to keep the social tone warm, it builds rapport.
3. Sales people are notoriously proud of their cars. A little friendliness will never go amiss.
4. We're both in the Rotary club. This means that we have something in common and something to talk about. Both are a real advantage.

Tactics and Counterplays

You need to be aware of the tricks of the trade. Use them at your discretion but above all be aware of when they are being used on you!

- **Personal history**
  Keep a keen record of the other party's personal history. Use it wherever possible. Information is power. Salespeople often do this, buyers rarely do so.

- **Well known phrase or saying**
  Check to see if the other side have any habits or customs worth remembering. Listen to their words. Do they have any favourite expressions that you could use back to them? Expressing things in the same style of language builds rapport, for example someone frequently using 'I see what you mean' could be someone who tends to think pictorially. Replay with 'Let me show you how my proposal would look'.

- **Clean and tidy**
  Your personal hygiene and dress tell much about you. Never be caught out in this area.

- **Shake hands**
  A poor handshake can cost you thousands of pounds. Practise a good firm grip if necessary.

- **Shared experiences**
  Try to find at least two things that you and the other party have in common. Once discovered mention them regularly in conversation but don't overdo it.

Exercises

We all know exercises are important. They keep you fit and ready to negotiate. Think of real examples and try to relate our theory back to your own experience.

1. If you started to keep more rigorous records of your opposition negotiators, what would be your starting points?

2. Think of your largest client/supplier. What personal habits do their negotiators have? Do they have any company customs or jargon? How might you use these ideas to your advantage?

Negotiation Dilemmas

Here is an opportunity to test your knowledge against a set of difficult scenarios. What would you do in these situations? You can read our ideas after you have written your own.

Dilemma 13
The other party makes a particularly offensive, racist remark and finishes it with 'don't you agree?' You are horrified. How do you react?

OUR VIEW

This is a tough problem because whatever you say you could be in a difficult personal situation.

It would be poor from a moral standpoint meekly to acquiesce. On the other hand there may be little to be gained by antagonizing the other party gratuitously. Of course, the comment is unacceptable but you are not the keeper of the other person's morals and this may not be the best place to have a discussion on the subject.

To the question 'don't you agree?' you should offer a non-inflammatory comment such as 'Lets talk about that another time', and move on. You know how you feel personally. Silence may also be another option.

It is worth remembering several clips of vocabulary that can get you out of difficult situations. The comment 'interesting' covers a multitude of sins and does not commit you one way or the other. It is the comment of a good poker player. Find some comments of your own and use them to dodge situations that could prove difficult.

It may be the case that the behaviour of the other party is so unacceptable that you may start to reconsider the deal. If what you have experienced is symptomatic of the person or company as a whole you may indeed be doing the correct thing, by thinking about the value of continuing to do business with such a person or company.

Negotiation Dilemmas

Here is an opportunity to test your knowledge against a set of difficult scenarios. What would you do in these situations? You can read our ideas after you have written your own.

Dilemma 14

As you walk into the room you are faced with a particularly attractive member of the opposite sex who immediately makes it clear that they are 'interested' in you. How do you react?

OUR VIEW

Commercial negotiations should always take place in a warm and friendly atmosphere but as with all things there are lines to be drawn.

If you find that you are being targeted then the first issue is to be aware of it and see it from a negotiation perspective. As with the previous dilemma you cannot be held responsible for the personal moral views of the other party.

Professional behaviour should not allow you to do or say anything that would be considered improper and the first move here is to make it clear (as politely and professionally as possible) that you wish to progress the business and move on. You can invent another appointment and refrain from any small talk.

The penny will soon drop even if it is at the expense of the warmth of the meeting. This may be an occasion where some coldness may be appropriate.

If the behaviour continues you may seek to find a substitute who could replace you or, as before, you may question your desire to continue the business.

Should the behaviour be completely unacceptable you should not jeopardize your own personal standards. It may be appropriate to mention that the behaviour is offensive and that you do not wish to continue. How far you make your feelings known to the other party is a tactical decision based on personal knowledge of the individuals and companies concerned.

Care is needed that you have judged the situation correctly. Rejection handled badly can create an enemy.

Just Before you Finish

List up to three things that you intend to do differently as a result of this step.

1.

2.

3.

Step 8   The power of questions

Information is crucial to the outcome of a negotiation and you should take the initiative with a well practised and thorough questioning technique. Not only will appropriate questioning provide you with information but the phrasing and skill used should stimulate a more open exchange of views.

OPEN QUESTIONS

These questions usually begin with words such as Who, Why, What, How, When, and Where. They cannot be answered with a simple yes or no – they demand more. The onus is then on you to listen to the answers (see Step 9). Expert negotiators understand the power of open questions especially during the opening of the negotiation.

Open questions	Appropriate for	Not appropriate
'How can we help you?'	Encouraging discussion.	When you need to be more specific.
'What are your reasons for . . . ?'	Gaining more information.	

CLOSED QUESTIONS

Closed questions usually demand a simple yes or no answer. They are useful for establishing specific points of fact and can assist in summarizing – when you are going through various points to clarify the situation or what has been agreed.

Closed questions	Appropriate for	Not appropriate
'Can you deliver by the 17th?'	Checking specific facts. Clarifying the situation.	Gaining general information.
'Is this what you suggested?'		If you do not want a no answer.
'Have we got a deal?'		

Closed questions are often asked at the conclusion of the negotiation. The ultimate closed selling question is 'Will you buy it?' and this is the reason why salespeople avoid closed questions so readily.

If you ask a closed question in a sales environment and receive a positive reply, then the problem is solved. If, however, the answer is 'no' then you are at a disadvantage. Only ask a closed question if you can live with a negative answer. You may prefer to follow the route of salespeople and try to close the other party with an alternative method. The choice would be 'How much discount can you give me'? rather than 'Can you give me a discount?'

PROBING QUESTIONS

Such questions are usually used to clarify points of detail and are normally open questions directed to a specific subject. Some excellent probes are not actually questions but statements such as 'Please, tell me more.' You can choose whether to probe by making a statement or by asking a question that can validate or expand on the information you already have.

Probing questions	Appropriate for	Not appropriate for
'What specific tests do you use to ensure consistent quality?'	Checking information already obtained. Tying down the other party and making them give you the information you require.	If exploring personal information – care will be needed.
'Why do you say that?'		
'What exactly happened last time?'		

LEADING QUESTIONS

Leading questions – indicate the answer that is expected.

Leading questions	Appropriate for	Not appropriate for
'So there will be no problem in meeting our quality requirements?'	Gaining acceptance of your views.	Obtaining information on how the other party feels.
'These prices will remain fixed for 12 months, won't they?'		

REFLECTIVE QUESTIONS

Such questions are a powerful means of expressing your own, and obtaining information about the other person's, feelings. They often appear as statements without a question mark, but clearly require a response from the other person indicating how they feel.

Reflective questions	Appropriate for	Not appropriate for
'You seem unhappy about that proposal.'	Encouraging the other person to continue talking and to look deeper into a situation.	Checking facts.
'That seems to cause you a problem.'		

It is relatively easy to phrase closed questions and they can be very effective in establishing facts and information. Open questions can be seen as encouraging discussion and seeking the other person's opinions in an unprejudiced way. You should attempt to use a combination of types of questions at different points of the negotiation. For example:

> Seller – 'I believe you were late in payment for the last order we delivered. Is that correct?' (closed)
> Buyer – 'Yes.'
> Seller – 'What were the reasons for this?' (open)
> Buyer – 'We had some staffing problems within our accounting systems department.'
> Seller – 'You feel that things were particularly difficult at that time.' (reflective)
> Buyer – 'Yes, a couple of systems had failed and we hadn't got the appropriate staff to deal with it.'
> Seller – 'So what did you do about it?' (probing)

Effective questioning skills involve asking the appropriate questions at the appropriate times. Excessive use of closed questions, for example, may close the meeting down at the very point where you want to encourage the other person to talk about a particular issue.

HYPOTHETICAL QUESTIONS

Hypothetical questions are another powerful type of question which can be used to good effect in a negotiation. These questions usually begin 'What if . . .' or 'Suppose . . .' They are useful for getting the other party to think about new ideas, and are especially helpful in breaking deadlock situations.

They enable various options to be tabled for discussion but free from any commitment, for example:

> 'What if we extended the contract to two years?'
> 'Suppose we made you our sole supplier?'

Creativity is a powerful tool and characterizes the skilled negotiator. Hypothetical questions provide one way of introducing creativity.

MULTIPLE QUESTIONS

These are usually a string of questions asked as one, for example:

> 'How do you ensure fixed prices, delivery, quality and the level of after-sales service we require?'

Multiple questions are useful for putting the other party under pressure – but make sure that you get *multiple* answers. Often the other party will just sit back and answer the part of the question – usually at length – that suits them best.

If you ask each question separately it will carry more weight and will force the other party to answer each part in turn.

STEP 8   KEY POINTS

1. Plan your questions in advance.
2. Concentrate on open questions at the beginning of meetings.
3. When you find something interesting - probe.
4. Make sure that you write down all important facts.
5. If you want commitment ask a closed question.

Negotiation Scripts

Which of the following scripts are useful and positive? Which should be avoided? Suggest reasons why and then compare your ideas with ours.

1. So how's business, these days?

2. Where do you source your raw materials?

3. That sounds interesting. Tell me more about it.

4. That's a key point. I hope you won't object if I make a few notes.

5. Right then, Paul, have we got a deal?

6. Now, was it the red or the blue that you wanted?

OUR VIEW

1. Salespeople use this question almost as a greeting. It's about the most popular open question. Try to be original and find something that sounds more authentic.
2. An excellent open question. You are seeking information. Too many of such questions can sound like an inquisition but it's a good start.
3. A non committal reply followed by a question. Good negotiation tactics.
4. Write down important points. It shows the other party that you are listening to what they are saying.
5. A closed question. Be careful because the answer might be 'no'.
6. An alternative to a closed question. You have not given the other party an opportunity to decline. It moves you closer to the ultimate decision on the deal.

Tactics and Counterplays

You need to be aware of the tricks of the trade. Use them at your discretion but above all be aware of when they are being used on you!

- **Closing in**
  When you're selling be careful with closed questions. Try some alternatives.

- **Looking for problems**
  If you are a buyer tell the other side that everything is going well. They will be looking for problems. If you haven't got any it's difficult for them to sell you their product or service.

- **Fifteen all!**
  You can always answer a question with a question. 'You'll have to lower your prices' can be followed by 'How important is price to you compared with quality, let's say?'

- **It's good, isn't it?**
  Use question tags. 'This is quite a new development, Mr Smith, isn't it?' As you say 'isn't it' look the other party in the eyes and nod your head. They will be drawn by your behaviour to agree with you.

- **Silence is golden**
  When you've asked a powerful question always be quiet and give the other party time to reply. Silence is an important issue. Don't fill it with your own words or be embarrassed by its use.

Exercises

We all know exercises are important. They keep you fit and ready to negotiate. Think of real examples and try to relate our theory back to your own experience.

1. Write down three questions you are determined to ask at your next negotiation.

2. List one open question, one probe and one closed question that concern the subject of price.

Negotiation Dilemmas

Here is an opportunity to test your knowledge against a set of difficult scenarios. What would you do in these situations? You can read our ideas after you have written your own.

Dilemma 15

The other party in the negotiation ask 'Well, Chris so what do you think of our new specification and pricing policy?' How do you reply?

OUR VIEW

Not every salesperson you meet will give you such a fine opportunity. This is a particularly unskilful question because it has given you the initiative to reply in such a way as to give you significant leverage. You can choose from the luxury of two different approaches: the first is to sound pleased; the other to look miserable.

With the first approach you can say that you are mightily impressed with their new spec and pricing policy and with only one or two minor modifications you can see no reason why you should not be taking advantage of the package. Of course, your opinion and theirs concerning the size of a 'minor' modification may well differ.

The second approach is to look at the other party and say that unfortunately you are not particularly impressed with what they have offered you and if they want your business they will have to do a lot better than that. This is quite a dismissive approach but does show that you may be able to do business.

You can also use this as an opportunity to tell the other side what exactly you think of their offer in detail and you can use your logic to get your reasons in first.

All in all you have the advantage. Make sure that you make full use of it.

Negotiation Dilemmas

Here is an opportunity to test your knowledge against a set of difficult scenarios. What would you do in these situations? You can read our ideas after you have written your own.

Dilemma 16
A salesperson says to you 'Look, Mrs Jones, you ordered six last month. Shall I put you down for another six or would you prefer to get the extra discount for buying eight? Which do you prefer?' How can you gain the initiative?

OUR VIEW

This is an example of the alternative close and is most popular with salespeople, mainly because it works so well!

You will now know how powerful closed questions can be. In this dilemma the closed question has been substituted with a choice. Obviously you are supposed to say 'when' you want something and 'how many' you will want rather than if you want them.

Your reply here is to make it very clear that the question is 'if' rather than 'how many'. You should state that you may indeed be very happy to place a large order if the price (and any other variable you care to mention) is significantly lowered.

Bounce the tactic straight back with the comment 'Right, tell me about your discounts then. Can you do 10 per cent with 90 days terms or is it 60 days that you prefer?' Look them straight in the eyes and listen for the response.

Just Before you Finish

List up to three things that you intend to do differently as a result of this step.

1.

2.

3.

Step 9 The skill of listening

There is little point in asking open questions and probing deeply if you are not listening carefully for the answers at the same time.

Expert negotiators know how important it is to practise good listening skills. These are skills that can be learned and used. Hearing is not listening. Listening needs effort and can be hard work.

ENCOURAGE THE OTHER PARTY TO TALK

The more that people talk the more they give away. A good listener is able to gather a great deal of information when confronted by a talkative person across the table. Encourage them to talk.

Remember also what represents many people's most popular subject – themselves! People will talk endlessly about their hobbies, families, car, holidays, etc. if prompted. All of this information may prove useful. Keep a record of what is said (even to the point of maintaining a file on each contact you deal with).

HUNT DOWN THE MISUNDERSTANDINGS

As you listen to the other side you will soon hear if there have been any misunderstandings during the first minutes of your negotiation. It may be that one of your assumptions has proved faulty or that the other party have the wrong information. Do not hesitate to correct these errors and be open and honest. There is little point in continuing a discussion if it is based on a faulty premise and cannot be taken to a proper conclusion.

ACTIVE LISTENING SKILLS

- Listen to what others have to say in order to understand what they mean.
- Listen to what others have put into their idea (look for the positive).
- By listening you are more able to identify skills in other people.
- By listening you are able to gain a clearer picture of what is in somebody's mind so you are able to respond.
- When listening put your own thoughts to the back of your mind in order to understand the other person's point of view.
- By attentive listening you are able to make better use of time by quicker understanding.

- Lack of listening will demotivate others, particularly where the boss doesn't listen.
- By listening you will be able to recall valuable information.
- By listening you show consideration and respect for others.
- By listening you can gain or improve your authority.
- By listening you will improve the level of influence you have.

SOME BEHAVIOURS THAT INDICATE LISTENING

Reflecting	Let me see if I've got your point . . .
	Are you saying . . . ?
Supporting	Yes, good idea.
	And then?
Disagreeing	Won't that cost too much?
Constructing	Would it help if we . . . ?
	What would you like to happen?
Criticizing (but carefully!)	If we do this for him, we'll have to do it for everybody else.
Clarifying	Isn't the point that . . . ?
Interpreting	Are you suggesting . . . ?
Confirming	So, we agree that . . .
Testing	Would it be right to say that . . . ?
	If we did this, then . . .

Characteristics of listening

Ineffective	Effective
Non-verbal behaviour	
Listener looks bored, uninterested or judgmental; avoids eye contact; displays distracting mannerisms (doodles, plays with a paper clip, reads papers, etc).	Listener maintains positive posture; avoids distracting mannerisms; keeps attention focused on speaker; maintains eye contact; nods and smiles when appropriate.
Focus of attention	
Listener shifts focus of attention to himself; 'When something like that happened to me I . . . '	Listener keeps focus of her comments on the speaker: 'When that happened, what did you do? How did you feel?'
Acceptance	
Listener fails to accept speaker's ideas and feelings: 'I think it would have been better to . . .'	Listener accepts ideas and feelings: 'That's an interesting idea, can you say more about it?'

Empathy

Listener fails to empathize: 'I don't see why you felt that?'	Listener empathizes: 'So when that happened, you felt angry.'

Probing

Listener fails to probe into an area, to follow up an idea or feeling.	Listener probes in a helpful way (but does not cross-examine): 'Could you tell me more about that? Why did you feel that way?' Listener follows up: 'A few minutes ago you said that . . .'

Paraphrasing

Listener fails to check the accuracy of communication by restating in his own words important statements made by the speaker.	Listener paraphrases at the appropriate time.

Summarising

Listener fails to summarize.	Listener summarizes the progress of the conversation from time to time.

Advice

Listener narrows the range of alternatives by suggesting a 'correct' course of action.	Listener broadens the range of ideas by suggesting (or asking the speaker for) a number of alternatives.

THE POWER OF SUMMARY

One of the best listening skills is the use of summary. When you summarize you are checking your understanding and at the same time gaining control over the conversation.

Perhaps the best way to summarize is to repeat back to the other party what they have just said. If you use an expression like 'So what you are saying is . . .' you will be able to check that you have heard and understood the key points.

USING THE TELEPHONE

The principles of listening are even more important on the telephone. When eye to eye contact is broken the use of words becomes paramount.

Expert negotiators do not enjoy using the telephone to make important decisions. It is vital to be able to look into the other party's eyes at key moments. Our advice is to try to meet face to face wherever possible.

A strong case can stand up to an exchange of words but is sometimes diluted when negotiators can see each other. When two sides can see each other they tend to move together. On the telephone the stronger case can often prevail.

A telephone call is a useful means of conditioning the other party concerning a price rise or a change of expectations. As there is no eye contact it is easier to tell lies on the telephone so be careful that you are not manipulated into a difficult position by somebody who won't stop talking and let you interrupt. Interrupting is difficult on the telephone so be wary of the long speech.

Certainly, do not leave a telephone call without a thorough summary of what has been agreed. It is very easy to misunderstand what you thought you heard.

CONSIDER THE OTHER PERSON

It may well be that you are not immediately attracted by the quality, content or style of the other person. Never let this show. You must maintain a professionally positive outlook and keep the conversation moving.

Remember one of the key elements of negotiation: the more people like you the more they will give you; the more they dislike you the easier they will find it to say no.

THE POWER OF SILENCE

Never underestimate the power of silence. Be aware of the effect it can have on the other party if you sit and say nothing. It can be most threatening and difficult to endure.

A good maxim is to say nothing if you have nothing to say. Sit, listen, gain information and then ask questions. This will net you enormous advantages.

STEP 9   KEY POINTS

1. Look interested and encourage people to talk, especially about themselves.
2. Listening is an active skill that needs to be practised.
3. Make people feel that you are interested in them.
4. Use silence as a powerful conversational tool.

5. Use all of the listening techniques at your command.
6. Avoid the telephone wherever possible for important negotiations.

Negotiation Scripts

Which of the following scripts are useful and positive? Which should be avoided? Suggest reasons why and then compare your ideas with ours.

1. So how did your son get on in that match you were talking about the last time we met?

2. That sounds interesting. How long have you been involved with the Women's Institute?

3. Hold on a moment. My notes from the last meeting stated a February delivery date and not March. I think we must have had a misunderstanding.

4. Isn't it a small world. I was there recently myself.

5. 10,000 stamps you say. It must be quite a problem keeping track of them all.

OUR VIEW

1. Most parents enjoy talking about their children. If this comment is seen as a genuine attempt at creating a social arena then it will always prove useful. Be careful that it is not seen as being false and manipulative.
2. Encouraging people to talk about themselves is positive both socially and professionally. 'That sounds interesting' is a good phrase because it indicates you respect them and find their ideas interesting.
3. Good use of summary and note-taking. This could have been a genuine mistake or it could be more sinister. Be assertive and mention it.
4. You've shown that the two of you have something in common. This should make the conversation go well, and the subsequent business.
5. Don't show that you're not interested. Always be genuinely interested in people.

Tactics and Counterplays

You need to be aware of the tricks of the trade. Use them at your discretion but above all be aware of when they are being used on you!

- **Rubber ball**
  If you feel that you are being manipulated in a conversation then reverse the roles. Bounce it straight back with 'That's a good point. What do you think about it? I'm not too sure, myself.'

- **Time out**
  When you wish to find some time in the middle of a conversation that is going the wrong way, take a timeout. A visit to the toilet, perhaps, or the offer of a cup of coffee. It can break up the flow of argument or conversation.

- **Write on**
  Always make notes. It can be off putting if the other person immediately grabs a pen and says: 'That's really interesting. Let me make a note of this.' It makes people think that they may have given something away.

- **Let them talk**
  Remember that listening is always more powerful than talking. If you have

a talkative adversary, keep them going. The more people talk the more information you can gather.

- **In control**

  Questioning and listening offer control. As you are listening be ready with the next question and go straight ahead. This will give you the initiative in the conversation.

Exercises

We all know exercises are important. They keep you fit and ready to negotiate. Think of real examples and try to relate our theory back to your own experience.

    1. Write down three things you can do to improve your listening skills.

    2. Who is your most talkative customer or supplier? How can you now use good listening skills with them to increase your negotiation leverage?

Negotiation Dilemmas

Here is an opportunity to test your knowledge against a set of difficult scenarios. What would you do in these situations? You can read our ideas after you have written your own.

Dilemma 17

You are faced with a very low reactor who says absolutely nothing and seems to enjoy long silences. How do you react?

OUR VIEW

Low reactors are some of the hardest negotiators to meet across a table. The ability to sit and say nothing is truly a powerful weapon.

In most situations in a negotiation the more that you say the more that you give away. That is why questioning is such a useful technique. This, then, is the arena of the low reactor.

When silence is starting to become almost insufferable the low reactor seems to be able to sit there without feeling any discomfort or embarrassment. In any battle of nerves these people can sit poker-faced.

Once you have identified these attributes you can then begin to copy them. If you know that you are by nature a gregarious character you must curb your natural instincts to be talkative.

Experienced experts have a great deal of self-knowledge. They are aware of those traits that come naturally to them and those that require effort. You must seek to do the same. Know your strengths and weaknesses and when you come up against particular characters identify the situation and react accordingly.

Low reactors say little and enjoy silence. Be like them even if it feels uncomfortable. That will be your successful first move in the contest.

Be very careful of giving concessions. Consider a recess to assist you.

Negotiation Dilemmas

Here is an opportunity to test your knowledge against a set of difficult scenarios. What would you do in these situations? You can read our ideas after you have written your own.

Dilemma 18

The salesperson opposite is giving you the script that they learned on their last training course. They seem determined to continue right to the end. You are becoming bored and annoyed. How do you react?

OUR VIEW

When you are a buyer and know exactly what you want but the seller still seems to want to give you the full treatment, it can be most infuriating.

Salespeople can suffer from a rush of blood when they think that they are going for a major sale. Often this rush of blood can be counter-productive and can antagonize the buyer to the extent that they walk away.

This salesperson is diametrically opposite to the low reactor but needs special treatment just the same. You long to press the 'pause' button but to no avail.

You are in a much stronger position here than with a low reactor. You have the opportunity to reel in the information, store it and then use it back to your advantage. If the salesperson is inexperienced it may be that they are being quite indiscreet in offering you so much information.

If you feel that the negotiation is drifting you should interrupt and get the conversation back on target. It is not difficult to interrupt the most talkative person using an appropriate behaviour label followed up with a string of powerful questions.

You have the choice here whether to interrupt or sit and listen. Pick the one that will earn you the greatest amount of leverage in the rest of the sale or negotiation.

Just Before you Finish

List up to three things that you intend to do differently as a result of this step.

1.

2.

3.

6 MANAGING MOVEMENT

Step 10 Who moves first?

A great many definitions of negotiation contain the word 'movement'. A negotiation can involve movement or change towards an agreement that is seen as beneficial to each party.

This does not mean, however, that the process of movement has to be bilateral. Two-way movement is a perfectly proper process but the key point to make here is that you should only contemplate moving once you have exhausted the means by which you can get the other party to move on their own.

What we are searching for here are approaches that will cause the other party to move towards us before we have to consider moving towards them. There are three approaches or styles of negotiating that are likely to cause unilateral movement from the other party:

- emotion
- logic
- threat.

These were covered in the introduction and it may now be opportune to revisit your profile scores to check which of these three you use most often and more importantly, most effectively.

EMOTION

Emotion is a powerful means of moving people. Advertising agencies use it above all other methods to move us to making a purchase.

If you can arrange the feelings of the other party in such a way to cause them to move towards you then you have found the power of emotion. Words such as 'sympathy, love, envy, pity, delight, friendship and care are all associated with ways of leveraging some movement from others.

LOGIC

If you have a powerful argument and you time its use well you have every chance of persuading the other party to move unilaterally.

During the preparation phase you will have prepared your ideas, gathered evidence and been ready for counter-arguments so nothing here should take you by surprise. This is the opening stage of the negotiation and gives you the opportunity to state your case and offer your reasoning, evidence and statistical proof.

The key to this early stage of negotiation is to ensure that your case and logical reasoning take precedence. Make sure that you are saying 'why' before the other party are saying 'why not'. Get your reasons in first. It is more difficult to counter an argument when the other party have already gained momentum. Most will vigorously defend a position they take.

Accordingly never give the other side the chance to lay out their reasons and logical arguments. Be careful about asking the other negotiator 'why' they believe what they have said is true, or 'why' they are putting up their prices. All that you will receive is a barrage of justification from a well-prepared adversary.

You may well find that the other party will move unilaterally towards your position courtesy of your powerful and well-timed case of logical reasoning.

THREAT

Threat may be seen as the counter-balance to emotion. If emotion feeds on love then threat feeds on fear.

It may be possible to generate unilateral movement from the other side if they are sufficiently fearful of a negative outcome. This has to be done skilfully otherwise a great deal of bad feeling can be generated which can subsequently cause grief.

Subtle use of threat consists of the potential withdrawal of business, loss of opportunities, inability to sign a larger order. Quite often threat is cloaked in words such as: 'It would be a great shame . . .' or 'I hope that you won't make me . . .'

Always consider the subtle use of threat and rarely use it explicitly. It can be a powerful persuader but at the same time it needs careful implementation.

STEP 10   KEY POINTS

1. Try to make the other party move unilaterally.
2. Emotion, logic and threat are powerful means of one-way movement.
3. Be prepared and understand your case.
4. Get your logic in first.
5. Be careful asking the question 'Why?'
6. Threat needs careful handling.
7. Don't threaten people. Threaten deals.
8. Don't make threats that you are not prepared to carry out.

Negotiation Scripts

Which of the following scripts are useful and positive? Which should be avoided? Suggest reasons why and then compare your ideas with ours.

1. My boss will shoot me if I go back with a deal like this.

2. How would you feel if one of your suppliers came in with a 9 per cent price rise?

3. What I'd like to say right from the outset, Dave, is that I'm looking for a reduction next year not an increase.

4. I know this is important to you but let me just tell you why I can't afford it.

5. I'd like to stop you there a moment. I really must tell you why this won't work.

6. I know you've researched your case well but let me just repeat my main point again. I know that it represents the crux of the matter.

7. If you could only make the first move I'm sure I'd be able to reciprocate.

8. It would be a shame if we had to take our business elsewhere.

9. Look, RPI stands at 2.4 per cent. You can't argue with that.

10. Come on, John, we don't want to fall out over such a silly thing as this, do we?

OUR VIEW

1. Emotion can be effective if it can be used credibly. If it is said in a foolish and unprofessional way then it will prove wholly counter-productive. The other party will start to question your professional credentials rather than be a party to your tactic. If you do not possess the confidence or the 'acting' skills then it may prove better to leave this sort of comment to one side.

2. This is a fine means of trying to turn the tables on the other party. Trying to get them to argue with themselves or feel unhappy with their position can be a useful ploy. It is an implied means of expressing your unhappiness with the number involved.

3. The use of the name is a positive warm gesture (if it sounds genuine) and you are putting down a clear conditioning statement before the negotiation has gone too far. This is positive negotiating behaviour.

4. Get your logic in first. Make sure that you make your case before the other party gets a chance.

5. Similar idea to 4 above but with the excellent technique of interruption. Never be afraid to interrupt the other party if you feel that the tide of the negotiation is turning against you.

6. If you have one major point then don't be afraid to continue repeating it. Persistence is a virtue and you should insist on making your point. It is far better to repeat a good point than try to find a second and not so powerful argument.

7. You are encouraging the other party to move with the promise that you will reciprocate. If you have exhausted all of the possibilities in terms of one-way movement then by all means continue but do not be too hasty to move yourself before you are sure that you have covered all one-way movement arguments and techniques.

8. This is a threat. It is quite discreet but the meaning is clear. Be careful, the other party may call your bluff so don't say it unless you can counter a reply that says, 'Well, I suppose if you have to then there's nothing we can do.' You have a riposte which is to move immediately towards warm emotion and reinforce how much you wish to do business but on your terms and conditions.

9. You can't argue with facts. Well, perhaps you can but it is always a powerful statement to produce one solid number. There are ways around this with emotion or counter-logic but it does give you some short-term advantage.

10. More emotion and use of names. There is also an element of threat here that you may be prepared to fall out if necessary. A good compendium phrase which gives you control of the conversation.

Tactics and Counterplays

You need to be aware of the tricks of the trade. Use them at your discretion but above all be aware of when they are being used on you!

- **Evidence for the prosecution**
  Don't be impressed with computer printouts, statistics or thick documents. They can all be easily manipulated.

- **Excuse me**
  If you feel that the other side is about to make a telling point interrupt and get your retaliation in first. It can deflate their advantage.

- **Nice and nasty**
  Don't be taken in by the Mr Nice and Mr Nasty performance. One character may give you a hard time while his colleague 'can do you a favour'. It's a well-rehearsed routine.

- **Russian Front**
  Be careful of the 'Russian Front' tactic. The other party will present you with such an unpleasant scenario that anything else seems acceptable by comparison. Judge each offer on its merits. Don't allow comparisons to affect your views.

- **The hurry up**
  Don't let the salesperson give you 'standing room only'. If you are told that there is only one in stock, that the offer will only last until the end of the week just hold your fire. Deals done in haste are often regretted.

Exercises

We all know exercises are important. They keep you fit and ready to negotiate. Think of real examples and try to relate our theory back to your own experience.

1. Write down three things you can do to add some warm, professional emotion to your negotiations.

2. What are the tactics you should employ against an opponent who is totally persuaded by logic? For many professional buyers it is their key method of persuasion.

Negotiation Dilemmas

Here is an opportunity to test your knowledge against a set of difficult scenarios. What would you do in these situations? You can read our ideas after you have written your own.

Dilemma 19

A seller tells you that he needs just one more big order to win a month's holiday in the Caribbean. He asks for your help and tells you that he will be eternally grateful. How do you react?

OUR VIEW

You've met this problem before and you should now feel more at home dealing with people who wish to use emotion as a means of extracting movement from you. This does not mean that you should immediately become cold and frosty. There is an opportunity here and you can exploit it.

You have two cards to play. One is the foreign holiday for the seller; the other is the size of the order you can place. You would want a discount anyway for a large order. You are able to command an even bigger discount when you know that the order means so much to the other party.

The first reaction should be to ask some questions about the holiday. Try to find out the cost and importance. The more that you know the more you can use the information. How far from getting it is he? What does he require of you? Is your order vital or is this just another ploy?

Ultimately the answer lies in whether you are able to offer a larger order. You should not refuse just because of the circumstances. If you have the ability to place an order this may be the right opportunity and you can get the discount of a lifetime (you hope!).

So proceed with the business. Set your sights high and sell your volume to the seller for the highest discount you can get. Remember that desperate people pay desperate prices. In this case maybe a desperate seller will offer desperate discounts.

Negotiation Dilemmas

Here is an opportunity to test your knowledge against a set of difficult scenarios. What would you do in these situations? You can read our ideas after you have written your own.

Dilemma 20

A major supplier wishes to put up prices by 8 per cent because the pound sterling has dropped against the American dollar. Her figures seem to be correct. How do you counter the arguments?

OUR VIEW

We can assume here that the supplier is telling the truth and that the figures and situation are accurate.

We need therefore to counter the arguments and select the correct strategy. There are two ways in which we can start the discussion: the first is to use logic to counter the logic that the other party has just used; the second is to use emotion.

The logical response to this situation is to examine the rates of exchange to see if we can put forward a counter-argument. It may be that we can unpick the logic or find a flaw in the argument. It may be that we can find fresh logic which will counter the facts, figures and research that are being presented to us.

The problem starts to grow when we cannot find any real counter-arguments and must accept that what the other party says is in fact correct. This is when we can use emotion.

The emotional response to a request for a price rise is simple and straightforward: 'We'd love to be able to pay your new prices but we just cannot afford to.' There is almost no reply to this. If you can't pay then you can't pay. It places the onus on the other side to come up with a means around the problem. Of course, the underlying threat is that if you can't afford this supplier then you may have to find another.

The strategic position may be important here. Who needs whom the most? This could cloud the judgement but the two primary responses are to use logic to unpick the numbers and emotion to say you can't afford to pay.

Would they give you a price reduction if the currency movement was reversed?

Negotiation Dilemmas

Here is an opportunity to test your knowledge against a set of difficult scenarios. What would you do in these situations? You can read our ideas after you have written your own.

Dilemma 21

One of your largest customers puts a deal on the table and says 'Take it or leave it'. How do you react?

OUR VIEW

This is not a difficult problem to solve once we have got to grips with having enough confidence to look the other party in the eyes and say 'no'.

You are being pushed here and you need to have the assertiveness to fight back. It may be that you are unable to walk away because you need the product or service more than the other party but none the less the message you are giving if you meekly roll over is that every time they push you will give way.

You need to reply with a comment such as 'I'm sure we can sort this one out.' You need to find the common ground whereby you get the product and they get the sale.

You then have to move through a series of questions where you try to find why it is 'take it or leave it'. You need to see if this is really true or if it is just a ploy. It is significant whether the statement is made at the beginning of the negotiation or at the end. To use a ploy like this at the beginning would be remarkably unskilful and you should immediately question the credibility of the other party. It has more impact at the end when you have already explored all major possibilities.

You may need to take it if you have to but you should do so reluctantly and at the same time try to obtain another concession from the other side or at least be open about your situation. 'I'll have to take it this time, as you know, but I am unhappy about your tactics here.' This allows you to leave with as much credibility as you can muster and puts you in a stronger position next time.

Just Before you Finish

You've tried three ways to get the other party to move unilaterally. If this has worked you have done well but you also need to know how to make concessions yourself. That's what you'll find out in the next step. Before you move on write down one thing in this step that you think you can use in your next negotiation.

Step 11   It's your turn to move

PLACING THE MARKER

Once you have done your preparation well, you will know exactly what parameters you have for movement: both upper and lower levels. Normally you will go into a negotiation with some room to manoeuvre. It is difficult to do so with absolutely no room to move.

What is important now is to apply these parameters skilfully so that you don't have to walk away because you were unrealistic or pay too much because you started too high.

First, look at your numbers and calculate what your opening bid will be. It has to be aimed high enough to secure a good deal (the more you ask for the more you're likely to get) but not so high that your credibility will be damaged. Your knowledge of the market will help you to put down your first marker in the best place.

**Beware if you are a buyer or seller – how much
do you *really* know about the market?**

Once that marker is down it remains down and cannot be removed. You must, therefore delay placing the marker as long as possible and when you do place it, place it with care.

**When a car salesperson asks 'What do you want for
your car?', answer, 'What are you prepared to offer?'**

Do not even think of making an offer or placing a marker until you have exhausted all one-way movement possibilities.

Certainly you should try to force the other party to place their marker first. In a buying or selling situation the buyer always has the advantage in as much as the seller will have a price list or may have put down a price in the tender documents. You may be pleasantly surprised that their aspirations are less than you expected and you can tune your deal accordingly. Be prepared to experience a rat-a-tat:

> 'I need a discount.'
> 'How much are you looking for?'
> 'What can you offer me?'
> 'Give me a clue?'
> 'I don't know, you're the expert . . .'

This is the legitimate counterplay of two good negotiators. Obviously someone will have to put down a marker eventually but try to make sure it is not you.

HOW TO MOVE

Once you decide to move you must move only in the smallest of increments. Again, plan the size of the steps that you will take. Remember also that you must try never to move unilaterally. That's what you want the other party to do! If you move try to receive something in return for your move: 'If you do . . . then I will. . . ' is the script.

If . . . Then . . .

Once you move you have advertised the fact that you can move. You are also allowing the assumption that you may have more movement to offer. Therefore never give anything away for nothing. You must trade your moves, not give them away and always move in the smallest possible increments. These increments should also be in decreasing size. This acts as a disincentive to the other party to continue asking for more.

You must also remember that if there is no pressure to move then don't. Concessions are only valued when they are won. If you move too easily you are only encouraging the other party to raise their expectations for further movements.

WHEN THE OTHER PARTY MOVES

You should always promote in the other party a willingness to make concessions. Try to convince them that their current position is untenable, that they will not lose face if they do move, or that you may reciprocate the move yourself if they go first.

Thank and bank

When you are offered something in a negotiation get into the habit of immediately saying 'thank you' and moving on. It is discourteous not to thank someone for something which they have given you. It is also a common human trait that if someone looks or sounds ungrateful you are much more likely not to offer any more.

Even if what you are offered is not ultimately what you want, bank it and go for more.

If a concession is offered on something you don't want, encourage it, value it and then ask for a concession in the area you want to be in. Refusing a concession is poor practice.

BEST CONCESSION BEHAVIOUR

A concession presents you with three problems:

- Should I make it now?
- How much ground should I give?
- What am I going to get in return?

STEP 11   KEY POINTS

1. Plan your opening bid carefully.
2. Be reluctant to put your marker down first.
3. Move in small steps only and as creatively as possible.
4. Move only in reaction to a movement from the other party.
5. Try not to move on your own.
6. Never give anything away – trade it.
7. Always say 'thank you' and go for more.

Negotiation Scripts

Which of the following scripts are useful and positive? Which should be avoided? Suggest reasons why and then compare your ideas with ours.

1. I might be able to offer you a half per cent discount if you can increase your order. How much can you go to?

2. How much were you intending to pay?

3. What did you say your budget was?

4. I'm looking for a substantial discount.

5. Thanks for that discount. I might be able to help you here.

6. Look, anything is possible. Why don't you let me know the size of the order and I might be able to help you with the price.

7. I've already offered you half a per cent. I might be able to add another one as you've pushed me so hard but only if you can give me something in return.

8. Thanks for that. It's certainly a step in the right direction.

OUR VIEW

1. This has two parts. You are offering something in return for something, which is fine and you are also asking a good open question which forces the other party to respond. They may respond with a question of their own but in the short term you are leading.

2. A straightforward question requiring the other party to put down a marker. If this is asked of you, you must ensure that you reply with something like 'What were you looking for?' rather than put down a marker yourself.

3. Another simple 'marker'-seeking question. You may be lucky and they answer it.

4. The key word here is 'substantial'. It allows you to be demanding without putting an actual number down. Expressions like this are very valuable weapons in the negotiator's armoury.

5. You now own the discount. You have thanked and banked it and can now try to increase it.

6. You are asking them to go first. If they show you their volume then you will show them your discount. Good practice.

7. Move only in the smallest of increments and ensure that you receive something in return. Sound technique.

8. As in 5 above you have thanked and banked. Well done – now go for more.

Tactics and Counterplays

You need to be aware of the tricks of the trade. Use them at your discretion but above all be aware of when they are being used on you!

- **Straw issues**
  Have a list of things that will cost you nothing to give and bargain them for important items. You can talk up their value with effective use of emotion. Make a little seem a lot.

- **Let's be open**
  Be persistent with your demands to see the other party's marker. Once you've put down your first bid immediately demand to see the other party's. ('I've shown you mine, where's yours?')

- **Thank you for the furry dice!**
  Even if you are offered something in a bargain that you don't want, never refuse it. You might be able to trade it back later for something that you do want.

Exercises

We all know exercises are important. They keep you fit and ready to negotiate. Think of real examples and try to relate our theory back to your own experience.

1. Think of your last two negotiations. Who put their marker down first? How did you structure your opening bid?

2. What are the increments of movement that you employed in your recent negotiations? How large was your first move away from your opening bid? How would you change this next time?

Negotiation Dilemmas

Here is an opportunity to test your knowledge against a set of difficult scenarios. What would you do in these situations? You can read our ideas after you have written your own.

Dilemma 22

After a spell of exchanging information it seems that you are going to have to put down your marker first. How might you do this with minimum damage?

OUR VIEW

First of all, are you sure that you really have to put down the first marker? Try to avoid it but if it would damage your credibility to withhold the bid you will have to make the first move.

One way to minimize the damage is to place your marker hypothetically. You might use an expression like 'OK if you want a price I'll give you one but I don't think that you'll be very impressed.' Similar is 'I can give you a number but I know from what you've said that it's probably a little more than you wanted to pay.'

Comments like these allow you to put down a very high marker without damaging your credibility. If you call it a 'high bid' yourself you can agree with the other party and then offer 'Well, what did you have in mind?' This gives you an opportunity to get a number from them.

Once you have put down a marker, no matter how high or unacceptable, you have the right to ask the other party to match it with a bid of their own. It is then that the real negotiation begins.

Negotiation Dilemmas

Here is an opportunity to test your knowledge against a set of difficult scenarios. What would you do in these situations? You can read our ideas after you have written your own.

Dilemma 23

The other party in the negotiation tells you that just one small move from you will clinch the deal. Do you believe them and how do you react?

OUR VIEW

This dilemma hinges on two points. The first is the definition of the word 'small' and the second is whether you believe them.

'One small step' has become a famous phrase. You will need to ask what exactly they have in mind. Remember to ask here as it is vital to get them to define what they mean by 'small' before you put in your version. Size is often only a matter of opinion.

Once they have told you what it is you have to do to clinch the deal you can then progress. You may be pleasantly surprised and more than able to meet their demands.

Of course, the next point then becomes important. It may be that even when you have given them what they want they then try the Colombo tactic. This is when someone asks for 'just one more small thing' right at the end of a negotiation when you thought everything was agreed.

Be careful. Verify that if you meet the demand you really will have a deal. This will make it clear to the other party that they will damage their credibility if they do not then move straight to an agreement.

Just Before you Finish

List up to three things that you intend to do differently as a result of this step.

1.

2.

3.

Step 12   *Bargaining and dealing*

This is the part of negotiation with which most people are familiar. The fact that it comes as Step 12 in the expert process shows how wide the gulf is between the expert and the novice. It shows how reluctant the expert is to move.

THE LANGUAGE OF BARGAINING

Bargaining becomes a much easier process when an effective script is used. The key expression is 'if I do "x" for you, then I want "y" in return.' I give you something in return for what you give me. If you have planned it correctly then you will be giving the other party something that costs you little in return for something that they value greatly.

EXCHANGING VARIABLES

In Step 3 we looked at the price of variables and how they will affect the cost of the deal. You now have to trade them for what we hope is in excess of their value to you.

Do not exchange a variable without first attempting to value it from both sides. A good example is the trading of payment terms. If the other party have cash flow problems and a large overdraft they may be prepared to reward you much more than the cost of the money if you can pay them promptly. They will receive something that they value highly and will be prepared to reward you accordingly. It may be that you are a cash rich company for whom early payment is not important. You have therefore obtained a first class trade: extra discount in return for early payment. The other party is also happy because they have secured their cash flow.

You can then move on to the next bargain – in a complex deal the number of variables to be traded often reaches double figures. So the process starts over again: 'What will you give me if I can help you with . . .'

THANK AND BANK (AGAIN!)

Remember from the last step that you should never refuse anything offered to you. It may be that you are seeking a larger discount than the one offered or that the payment terms are not quite right but you should never reject anything outright.

It is important to learn a script that includes sentences like 'Thank you for that. It's certainly a step in the right direction', or 'Thank you for the discount. It's not quite what we need but I appreciate you making the move towards me.' Both of these statements give you ownership of what has been offered but also make it very clear that more is required.

If you reject something that is offered to you the other party can always take it back. You should encourage the other party to move because once they have moved it is much easier for them to move again.

Many times novice negotiators disdain concessions from the other side. If you have a sour expression and a rejecting tone of voice the concession will be withdrawn and the likelihood of you receiving something similar will be reduced.

BARGAINING WITH ONE VARIABLE

The settling of differences when there is only one variable at issue is known as compromise.

We saw with the early payment scenario that for bargaining to work successfully there has to be more than one variable. In that case it was two: early payment and extra discount.

When negotiation comes down to one variable and especially when there is likely to be a log jam with that last one a compromise becomes useful. It is the settling of differences within one set of parameters.

The best known and most obvious compromise is the 50:50 split. This is an easy way of settling differences. It is, however, almost too easy and is a soft option that expert negotiators avoid.

When faced with a potential compromise expert negotiators will demand far more than a mere 50:50 split. They will start at 99 to 1 and move from there. As was said with bargaining, never give anything away. Why give 50 per cent away just to settle the deal. Perhaps 10 per cent might settle it just as easily.

Compromise is a behaviour of last resort. When you use it be just as rigorous as you would be with any other part of the deal. Remember that a compromise favours the party that aims highest.

Compromise occurs most often in face-to-face negotiations and is not as readily used during telephone negotiations. One of the reasons for this is that it takes a lot longer to say something on a telephone. Hence, the negotiation is slowed down – compromises are normally quick.

STEP 12   KEY POINTS

1. Value the variables from both sides.
2. Try to give a little and get a lot.
3. When offered something say 'thank you' and go for more.
4. Find out what the other party needs most and make them pay for it.
5. Compromise as rarely and as late as possible.
6. 50:50 is not the only compromise.
7. Aim as high as possible at the beginning if you are possibly going to use a compromise approach later.

Negotiation Scripts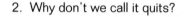

Which of the following scripts are useful and positive? Which should be avoided? Suggest reasons why and then compare your ideas with ours.

1. If you can give me six dozen I could give you 2 per cent discount.

2. Why don't we call it quits?

3. Let's split the difference.

4. Look, you know I need fast delivery. Bring it round tomorrow and I'll pay you COD.

5. What will you give me for cash?

6. Thanks for that move. I can see that we are going in the right direction.

OUR VIEW

1. A standard bargain. Common practice. Better still if a discount is offered but not an amount.
2. This is a sign of weakness. Compromisers are often too quick to concede. Avoid this type of comment. It shows that you are not a confident negotiator.
3. Why 50:50? Go for more and aim high.
4. Another trade-off. I'll do something for you if you do something for me. If you've priced it right it could be profitable.
5. Bargaining again. Be careful not to put down a marker and don't limit what you might receive.
6. Thank and bank. Show gratitude for what you've received, take ownership and go for more.

Tactics and Counterplays

You need to be aware of the tricks of the trade. Use them at your discretion but above all be aware of when they are being used on you!

- **Don't blink first**
  The side that suggests a compromise first may well be the weakest. Avoid it yourself and go for broke when it's suggested to you. (How about 99:1?)

- **Confusion**
  Be well prepared and at the right moment throw a large number of variables on to the table: 'If you can give me the extra volume with the free delivery then I might be able to give you the payment terms you want but only if you can package it for me.' This complication can confuse the poorly prepared. If it happens to you call a timeout immediately or admit that it is complicated and ask for a recap.

- **Something for nothing**
  Always have available one or two things that will cost you nothing which you could give as a sign of goodwill or better still trade for something valuable.

Exercises

We all know exercises are important. They keep you fit and ready to negotiate. Think of real examples and try to relate our theory back to your own experience.

1. Write down the most important variables that you use most often. How often are you able to put a value on them?

2. What do your main customers/suppliers consider to be the most valuable part of the deal? What variables do they normally want to discuss first? Can you think why?

Negotiation Dilemmas

Here is an opportunity to test your knowledge against a set of difficult scenarios. What would you do in these situations? You can read our ideas after you have written your own.

Dilemma 24
You are reaching a log jam in the negotiation and the other party offer to split the difference so that you can move on. What are your options?

OUR VIEW

You are 'reaching a log jam.' This means that you have been in the process for some time and are not at the beginning of negotiation.

At this stage it is easier to contemplate a compromise than at the beginning. To suggest a compromise at an early stage is a sign of weakness. Also, at this later stage one of the benefits of a compromise is that it can unlock what seems to be a firmly closed door.

You now have to decide whether a compromise will win you more than you might get if you try another approach. If you have exhausted other methods a compromise may be your way to a conclusion.

Immediately start to reassess your targets for the deal. A compromise approach will benefit the party that aims highest. Can you move your targets without damaging your credibility?

Once you have satisfied all of these criteria for planning, go ahead and start the process. Good luck!

Negotiation Dilemmas

Here is an opportunity to test your knowledge against a set of difficult scenarios. What would you do in these situations? You can read our ideas after you have written your own.

Dilemma 25

You know that the other party is cash rich. How can you structure the bargaining process to capitalize on this?

OUR VIEW

If you know that the other party is sitting on a pile of cash you have some very important information which you can use to your benefit. You know that they will not be saddled with cash flow problems and should be good payers. You can assess the benefit of dealing with them and proceed accordingly.

If you are a salesperson you may presume that they will be able to pay for your product more quickly, perhaps even 'Cash With Order', and for that you could reward them with a discount.

Start to plan for a series of variables that will suit both them and you. If they don't need cash, is there anything that they do want? What interests and concerns do they have that you could address providing that they use their cash to reward you according to what it is that you need?

Putting yourself in the other person's shoes is a very useful part of planning. It is too easy to think that because you know how you would feel if you had plenty of cash then this is how the other party must feel. Move round to the other side of the table. Have a look at what it is that they need, then start to prioritize and price both your and their variables accordingly.

Just Before you Finish

You've started the process of movement and have extracted concessions from the other side. How much more do you think they can give before the pot is empty? That's what you'll find out in the next step. Before you move on write down one thing in this step that you think you can use in your next negotiation.

Step 13 The edge of the cliff

ACES OR DEUCES?

As you move towards the end of the negotiation it soon becomes obvious that it is time to reach a conclusion. This may be an agreement or it could be a `walk-away'. Sometimes the end becomes clear because the size of the concessions being offered and traded becomes smaller and smaller.

At this stage you have to ascertain whether the other party has any more room to move or are, in fact, standing on the edge of the cliff ready to fall over. They may be calculating the same for you.

Watch out for brinkmanship. You can never be sure whether the other player is bluffing.

Your task then is to convince the other side that you have given them all that is on offer and if that is not sufficient either you will have to walk away or they will have to moderate their target.

You can add to your leverage by using a range of tactics to convince the other side of your inability to move:

1. I've exceeded my authority
You can find a series of reasons why you can't move any further. Blame your low budget this year, the bank manager, company policy, etc.

Be very careful that you do not mention your boss. To do so leaves you open to the other party suggesting that they talk to your boss directly. It also undermines your authority and credibility in being able to agree the deal.

2. This will cost me my job
Use emotion to persuade the other side that you have already gone further than you should have. This has to be done skilfully otherwise you can harm your credibility.

3. I'll have to reduce my order
Don't try to obtain any further movement from the other side. You reduce what you can offer in return for what they have put on the table.

Success in this area of negotiation always conditions the other party to accept what is on the table and to be satisfied that they could not have achieved any more.

STEP 13   KEY POINTS

1. When you plan always know how far you can go. Don't be carried away in the heat of the moment.
2. Always try to know how far the other party can move. Where is their real walk-away position?
3. Try to convince the other player that you have exhausted your store of concessions and that you are unable to move any further.

Negotiation Scripts

Which of the following scripts are useful and positive? Which should be avoided? Suggest reasons why and then compare your ideas with ours.

1. The cupboard is empty. There's only crumbs left.

2. I'd love to give you the discount but company policy won't allow me.

3. I've tried to tell the bank manager but you know what they're like.

4. Come on, Neil, just one more small move wins you the contract.

5. I understand your position. If you can't move on price I'll just have to reduce my order.

OUR VIEW

1. You have to be able to use such expressions carefully. You can make yourself look foolish and undermine your credibility if your 'cabaret' becomes too strong. None the less do include some expressions in your repertoire that offer a figurative and colourful view of your position. 'Crumbs left' indicates there is still movement to be had. Your 'crumbs' could be valuable to the other side.
2. You've placed the burden of blame on a third party and you have left yourself in the position of friend rather than enemy. Remember not to allow the other party any comeback by trying to change policy or speak to your boss (which should be your comeback if this script is tried on you).
3. This is rather manipulative and can leave you open to the reply 'Perhaps I ought to have a word with him', or similar. Probably one to avoid.
4. This is a fairly useful sentence. You have used the name to keep it friendly and have made it clear that you will respond with a carrot if they move. Of course, the problem here is the definition of the size of the word, 'small' – it would be more useful without it.
5. This offers a negative consequence of the inability to provide what you wanted. It is a threat and you should ensure that you are prepared to fulfill it if required. If you are bluffing then it could put you in a difficult position.

Tactics and Counterplays

You need to be aware of the tricks of the trade. Use them at your discretion but above all be aware of when they are being used on you!

- **Let me have a word with them**
  When the other party use a lever against you, destroy it immediately. Policy can be changed, offer to help them write to the bank manager, offer to speak to their boss.

- **Where's my coat?**
  Try a dummy 'walkaway'. Stand up and put your coat on. Tell them that unfortunately you can't win them all. It might provoke some more movement. You can do this only once.

- **Call my bluff**
  Don't buckle when faced with an ultimatum. It is probably true that they need this deal as much as you. Do not be afraid to hear tough words at

this stage and wade through them. Ask yourself if they would really walk away. Remember that if they ever move on a 'final' offer then their credibility will be seriously diminished.

Exercises

We all know exercises are important. They keep you fit and ready to negotiate. Think of real examples and try to relate our theory back to your own experience.

1. Think of a recent negotiation where you think that you left money on the table. How can you avoid it next time?

2. Think of some ways in which you might be able to test for the exact edge of a cliff. Is it an art or a science?

Negotiation Dilemmas

Here is an opportunity to test your knowledge against a set of difficult scenarios. What would you do in these situations? You can read our ideas after you have written your own.

Dilemma 26

At a crucial stage the other side look you in the eyes and say 'Well, that's it, Tom, it's either a handshake or I'm going to have to leave.' What is your reply?

OUR VIEW

This is 'take it or leave it' by another name and you should feel confident now at handling this.

- Is the other party really likely to walk away?
- Is this really the edge of the cliff?
- Is their ability to offer concessions really exhausted?
- Have you really pushed them as far as they can go?
- Who needs this deal most?
- Will you really give in or are you prepared to walk away?

These are the concerns that you have. You will never know if the other party are telling the truth or bluffing. Are they holding aces or deuces? Why not hedge a bit and see what you can find out: 'Come on, Fred, you're not really going to walk out when we're so close to a deal. I'm sure that we can sort this out.'

Don't make it seem that you are afraid that they might walk out but by the same token use warm emotion to show that a walk out would not be something that you, yourself, would want to encourage.

The inclination is that there is still some more money left on the table. Take some time to see if you can find it without falling over the edge of the cliff.

Negotiation Dilemmas

Here is an opportunity to test your knowledge against a set of difficult scenarios. What would you do in these situations? You can read our ideas after you have written your own.

Dilemma 27

The negotiator opposite reaches across the table and shows you a fax from her boss saying that she must not offer more than a 2 per cent discount. How do you react?

OUR VIEW

You've had several dilemmas now where you have had to try to ascertain whether the other party is telling the truth or just using a tactic. This is another example so we need to examine both sides of the situation.

If the boss really has prevented her from moving on the 2 per cent you have a fine reply. `Why don't I have a word with your boss', is the obvious riposte. The other party has, in fact, quite seriously undermined their position by revealing that they do not have authority to finalize the deal without referring back. Why deal with the monkey when you could deal with the organ grinder?

Expect a range of responses to this approach but you will have taken the initiative and can feel that you've moved forward by putting pressure on the other party.

The same comment would apply even if the other party were merely using this as a ploy. Either way they would be most reluctant to let you anywhere near their boss and would look for means of extricating themselves. Watch out for suggestions that they might be able to have a word with the boss on your behalf and insist again that you meet the boss.

A key point here is to beware using a tactic that can backfire badly. Plan the tactics that you think are appropriate but ensure that you fully allow for all the possible consequences.

Just Before you Finish

List up to three things that you intend to do differently as a result of this step.

1.

2.

3.

7 THE END OF THE ROAD

Step 14   Shaking hands

As the end of the negotiation moves into view you need to be prepared either to make an alternative offer or to accept the offer on the table. This presumes that you haven't decided to call it a day, i.e. go elsewhere.

In the sales environment this is the most important phase. The seller has worked through the sales process and now has to 'close'. This is the aspect of selling most written about and feared. It is the moment of truth when the customer says, 'yes' or 'no'.

Sales people are taught how to close out the deal. Buyers are less well trained but protect themselves with processes that stop the seller from reaching this stage. Tendering allows the buyer to choose which deal to take unencumbered by the pressure of an enthusiastic salesperson or a negotiation.

Generally the fast shaking of hands favours the seller. Salespeople wish to make the deal and get out before any second thoughts can interfere. Ultimately, whichever side you are on if you think that it is time to agree it is better to say so and shake on the deal. Unfortunately some buyers suffer from endless doubts and these can cause the loss of a good deal.

HARD SELL, HARD DEALS

Pressuring people may be fine in the one-off sale and negotiation but there is little point in tricking someone into making a potentially poor deal if you have to visit them again the next week or month.

Once people have had a chance to reflect on a deal they will soon form an opinion of whether it was to their advantage or not. If they feel that they have been tricked or manipulated they will become resentful and will seek to annul the deal or look for revenge the next time the business opportunity arises.

Good long-term relationships must be at the forefront of every deal. Treat people with respect and they will be happy to deal again.

WRITTEN EVIDENCE

No matter how professional the negotiators, the deal must be recorded on paper. It is at this time that misunderstandings will be ironed out and final numbers agreed. Details that were left 'on the backburner' need to be clarified and the final terms and conditions signed off.

It is always worth getting a fax or preliminary copy initialled as quickly as possible in order that final details are agreed.

MANAGING THE PEOPLE

At the final stages of a deal it is possible to strengthen relationships ready for the next round, next time. Never underestimate the importance of this stage. We have shown how first impressions can be important and the feelings at the end are equally so.

The other party should be thanked for their professional participation. You should, where appropriate, seek to offer some symbol of the agreement: buying lunch, a drink, or signing the deal with a commemorative pen. Make the other party feel good about doing business with you and happy about dealing with you personally.

No matter how well you believe the deal has gone you must never show triumph. Shouts of 'result!' as the pen hits the paper are not guaranteed to foster good lasting relationships!

Congratulate the other party on their professionalism. Flatter them a little and make them feel good about themselves. Again, as in many other sections of this book, we caution you to do this in a suitable and appropriate business manner.

Bear in mind that in any deal something that is not earned is not valued. Make the other party feel that they have had to work really hard to get the deal. They will value it more.

STEP 14   KEY POINTS

1. Don't trust to memory, write it down.
2. Make the final agreement a pleasant experience.
3. Make the other party, feel that they have 'earned' the deal.
4. Don't show triumph.
5. Try to build the basis for a long-term relationship if appropriate.

Negotiation Scripts

Which of the following scripts are useful and positive? Which should be avoided? Suggest reasons why and then compare your ideas with ours.

1. So, Christine, have we got a deal?

2. Let's just recap and write it down.

3. You're hard, but I might just be able to afford it.

4. A condition of this deal is that it must remain confidential. If anyone else wanted these terms it would be impossible to accommodate them.

OUR VIEW

1. Warm use of name and a push towards an answer. At the end of a deal you may have to use closed questions in order to test the level of commitment. Used properly these will allow you to test the temperature and obtain a firm view.
2. Summary is a very powerful form of control in a negotiation. By summarizing yourself, either verbally or on paper, you keep control of the agenda and can ensure that there are no misunderstandings.
3. Again, don't use this type of comment unless you are sure that you can put it in the right tone. It would be patronizing and unprofessional if you said this incorrectly. Said well it adds a little humour and can help create a warmer relationship.
4. A conditional offer. If the other party accept these terms you have a deal.

Tactics and Counterplays

You need to be aware of the tricks of the trade. Use them at your discretion but above all be aware of when they are being used on you!

- **Let's shake**
  Put your hand across the table when you wish to close the deal. The other party then have to refuse to shake if they want to continue negotiating.

- **Better on paper**
  Absolutely insist that you write up the deal prior to signing. It is quite common for mistakes to appear in a draft typed by the other party. Always gain control of minutes and notes.

- **Colombo**
  We have mentioned this previously but this is a good time to try the 'one more thing' tactic, the Colombo ploy. Just as you are reaching the very end of a negotiation and are ready to agree put in one last small request. You might say to the other side 'That does include delivery, doesn't it?' You may gain this last concession if they fear jeopardizing the whole deal.

Exercises

We all know exercises are important. They keep you fit and ready to negotiate. Think of real examples and try to relate our theory back to your own experience.

1. How did you close the last major deal that you made? Did you consciously plan to make it a special occasion?

2. Was your last deal a fast one or a slow one? Think of recent deals, can you see any difference between those that were concluded quickly and those that took a long time?

Negotiation Dilemmas

Here is an opportunity to test your knowledge against a set of difficult scenarios. What would you do in these situations? You can read our ideas after you have written your own.

Dilemma 28

You have reached the final stage of the negotiation when the other party say 'We'll have to get this agreed by the boss. It should only be a formality, I'm sure.' What could be the potential problem here?

OUR VIEW

Beware, you could be heading for trouble. Bosses have a terrible tendency to want to prove that they can negotiate better deals than their staff. Once the boss gets hold of this deal you may find yourself having to renegotiate it with the boss and having to give a concession if only to massage the boss's ego.

Make your counterpart fully aware that the agreement they are passing to their boss is *a deal* and not open to renegotiation. Remember that here the other party is your ambassador so it makes sense to get them on your side and to get them to 'sell' the deal internally on your behalf. You may need to give them some ideas to use to persuade the boss to underwrite the deal without getting involved yourself.

You may decide, though, that it is altogether easier to keep one or two concessions up your sleeve so that if the occasion arises you do have something to give if you meet the boss.

Salespeople often underestimate how much support they need from the buyer to get the deal accepted internally.

Negotiation Dilemmas

Here is an opportunity to test your knowledge against a set of difficult scenarios. What would you do in these situations? You can read our ideas after you have written your own.

Dilemma 29

You have agreed a preliminary deal and a draft has arrived for initialling prior to a next meeting. You notice that it is riddled with small but significant errors in the other party's favour. What is your reaction at your next meeting?

OUR VIEW

First of all you have only yourself to blame for not ensuring that it was your side that drew up the paper work. Of course, it may have been that this would not have been appropriate so now you have to react.

Even if you feel that the other party have tried to trick you, you must react as if all of the mistakes were genuine errors. In fact they may indeed be genuine, so tread carefully.

One by one the errors have to be revealed. The other party can hardly be surprised that you have scrutinized the document and probably they are waiting for your response.

If you feel that the errors were in fact put in to deceive you, you should look carefully at the whole deal and ask yourself if this is the type of company with which you would like to do business. It may be that you can use the errors to extract yourself from a deal that you are regretting entering into in the first place.

There is no room for deception like this in a negotiation. There is a place for the use of genuine tactics but what you are encountering here is potential fraud. If necessary call the deal off and walk away, allowing, of course, for any legal consequences that may need resolving.

Just Before you Finish

List up to three things that you intend to do differently as a result of this step.

1.

2.

3.

Step 15   *Controlling and leading*

Step 15 looks at how an expert negotiator can take control of a negotiation. Assuming control will help to ensure that the right agenda is followed and that the environment is created whereby you can make your points effectively and limit the control exerted by the other party.

TAKING CONTROL

Control results from good preparation. You should have a clear route map of the negotiation: journey and destination. This will be achieved by having your questions prepared and using them wisely. It is questioning rather than making statements that provides control. Questions force the other party to listen and concentrate ready to respond. Unbroken statements allow them to switch off and relax.

BEHAVIOUR LABELLING

Preface your comments or actions with a statement that tells the other party to be ready for what is about to happen.

If you preface your question with, 'Let me ask you a question . . .' you are in fact saying to the other side 'I want you to listen. Please be quiet!' This is a most effective way to ask questions and ensures that they carry maximum weight.

This technique also allows you to interrupt the other side when they are talking with words like 'I wonder if I could interrupt you a moment. I'd like to ask a question . . .' If you combine this with stretching out your hand in an assertive way you will nearly always find the space that you are seeking.

INTRODUCE THE AGENDA

At the beginning of the negotiation, at the social phase, you should make the first move with comments that suggest that it is time to start and that you would also like to discuss certain issues first. Obviously these will be the ones that are most important to you. The other party will obviously wish for the same so negotiating the running order may be the first important step of the meeting.

If you progress with the assumption that your agenda is the obvious way forward you may find that the other side goes along with this.

TIME IS THE KEY

Ensure that you maintain control of the timespan of the negotiation. If the meeting is to last one hour then do not leave issues that are vital to you until it is too late to discuss them fully.

This is even more important when you visit another office and do not have total control over the environment. Do not allow the other negotiator to dictate terms merely because you are playing the away fixture. This is also important when negotiating abroad. Your journey times must be clear in your mind and you should not allow yourself to be manipulated.

PLAN THE BREAKS AND TIME OUTS

At any stage of a negotiation you always have the option to ask for a recess. This can be a genuine visit to the toilet, a need to clarify or make a calculation or a tactical ploy to disrupt the opposition.

Be aware of these breaks and if you have coffee booked for 10.30 then do not allow the coffee to arrive just as you are making your most important point. At the same time you should know that whenever the negotiation gets tough it is a legitimate response to ask for a time out to reconsider some numbers, call back to base or consult colleagues.

Manage the environment to your maximum personal benefit.

STEP 15   KEY POINTS

1. Have a list of questions ready and work through them.
2. Make it clear that you wish the meeting run to your agenda.
3. Learn and practise how to interrupt politely.
4. Preface questions and interruptions with a behaviour label.
5. Keep track of the time frame of the negotiation.
6. Use breaks and recesses to maximum effect.
7. Put your important points first on the agenda.

Negotiation Scripts

Which of the following scripts are useful and positive? Which should be avoided? Suggest reasons why and then compare your ideas with ours.

1. Let me ask you another question if I may.

2. Shall we start, Mr X, there are a couple of preliminary questions I would like to ask.

3. I wonder if I could interrupt you a moment, John, there's a question I would like to ask.

4. We've only a short time left, Angela, and I must ask this question before we finish.

5. I propose we take a short break, John.

6. I've a plane to catch at two so we'd better get down to the main points.

OUR VIEW

1. This is good use of a behaviour label and gives you control of the conversation and ensures that the other party is listening.
2. Another excellent means of using control techniques with a name to ensure friendly yet firm control.
3. The same technique.
4. You've prioritized your issues and you are ensuring that you cover all of your main points before the meeting finishes.
5. A good way of asking for a time out to achieve whatever you wish.
6. You're in control and you've told the other party that you wish to run the meeting according to your own agenda.

Tactics and Counterplays

You need to be aware of the tricks of the trade. Use them at your discretion but above all be aware of when they are being used on you!

- **Let me finish**
  Don't allow yourself to be interrupted when you wish to make a key point. It is easy to have your point devalued with a trivial interruption concerning the heating or the draft from the window.

- **It's my agenda**
  Put difficult issues back in the agenda so that the other party will not have enough time to make their case. Keep them under time pressure when they have a good argument to put forward.

- **Questions answered with questions**
  If you are asked a tough question reply with 'That's an interesting point, Mr Wilkinson. What prompts you to ask that?' You may just be able to side-track him from making a significant point and allow yourself some breathing space while he answers questions from you.

Exercises

We all know exercises are important. They keep you fit and ready to negotiate. Think of real examples and try to relate our theory back to your own experience.

1. Write down three ways in which you can ensure control of the next negotiation in which you participate.

2. How can a buyer create control against a seller? What might buyers do to gain control from sellers?

Negotiation Dilemmas

Here is an opportunity to test your knowledge against a set of difficult scenarios. What would you do in these situations? You can read our ideas after you have written your own.

Dilemma 30

You are constantly being interrupted by an argumentative adversary. This is causing you concern and the negotiation is beginning to stall. What do you do?

OUR VIEW

First we need to make some tactical decisions.

- Is the negotiation going your way?
- Is this person actually shooting themselves in the foot?
- Are you happy with the negotiation continuing in this fashion even though you find it unusual?

If the answer to these questions is 'no' then you need to do something about it. As usual there are a range of options. If you need to break into the conversation then try to drive in a wedge to allow this to happen. The best way is with a behaviour label – signal your intention to do something prior to actually beginning. In this example it would be something like 'I wonder if I could just break in for a moment, I'd like to ask a question?'

This sentence should be accompanied by a firm gesture, a smile and strong eye contact. This leaves the other party in no doubt about your serious intention. If they then ignore you, you must have the assertiveness to continue and make it clear that you do not intend to back down on this point.

Have your questions arranged in advance. It will allow you to fire them off at key moments so that you gain control of the conversation. Most people feel the need to answer a question when one is asked, which allows you to drive the conversation in the direction that you desire.

You could also use emotion and let the other party know that you feel the negotiation is not making the progress it should and that you both need to rethink the agenda or perhaps take a recess.

It is a recurring theme of this workbook that if you reward bad behaviour by the other party then all that you will receive in return is more bad behaviour. You must let the other party know that there is a downside to their poor behaviour. As always this must be said in an appropriately professional tone.

Negotiation Dilemmas

Here is an opportunity to test your knowledge against a set of difficult scenarios. What would you do in these situations? You can read our ideas after you have written your own.

Dilemma 31
You are in a difficult position and the tide is flowing against you. What options are open to you?

OUR VIEW

Much here depends on experience and confidence. If you have the ability to carry it off then you might try to be open and just a little theatrical and say something like, 'Look, I'm feeling hurt and attacked here. This is going to cost me millions and I'm not going to be able to continue if you keep trying to back me into a corner.'

If you do it correctly you may be able to get the other party to reply with 'Why, what's wrong?' which suddenly now puts you back in the action with a long piece of well-considered logic.

Another option is to go for an adjournment. It may be better to bring the meeting to a premature conclusion in order to regroup and rethink than to continue when things are going so badly. It may be that a shorter recess could help initially.

Why not try to put the issue 'on the backburner' so that you can get to an agenda that suits you. Obviously you cannot expect the other party to acquiesce to this but it may be worth trying. This shows the value of planning both your arguments before the negotiation and the running order of the agenda. Be aware that what you can do to the other party they can do to you.

Just Before you Finish

List up to three things that you intend to do differently as a result of this step.

1.

2.

3.

Step 16   The meaning behind the words

You cannot become an expert negotiator without an understanding of the power that words and language can have within a negotiation. Expert negotiators have the ability to choose and manipulate words to an extent that would surprise most ordinary negotiators.

TERMS AND CONDITIONS

There is no need to stress the importance of the effect that terms and conditions can have on the outcome of a negotiation. Knowing as we do that the price is not the cost, the loading of words within the terms and conditions can prove crucial.

A good example lies within the realm of payment terms. Think for a moment of the many ways in which a buyer can pay for a product or service:

- cash on delivery
- net monthly
- bank transfer
- pro forma invoice
- direct debit
- choice of currency
- extended terms (7–180 days)
- invoice by electronic data interchange (EDI)
- credit card.

These are just a few. They prove that a negotiation cannot be complete until every last word is agreed and signed off. 'We can give you favourable payment terms,' can mean many different things to many different people.

OUT OF THE MOUTHS OF BABES . . .

Expert negotiators routinely choose their words with utmost care. They have the ability to think in real time; to hear what is said and react immediately with their own careful choice of words.

Most expert negotiators hate having to say 'no'and will avoid anything that seems to close the door on a specific issue. If you work on the principle that anything is negotiable then you will be reluctant to rule something out. Therefore expert negotiators avoid negative words at all costs. Salespeople, especially, will not wish to walk away from a potential sale.

Here is a list of phrases that are often used to avoid saying 'no', and the real meanings that should be attributed to them.

Expert statement	Meaning
It would be almost impossible to move on that price.	There's more left if you care to ask for it.
As things stand it would be impossible to change our pricing.	We are flexible and can change if you push us hard enough.
We do not normally offer discounts.	We always give discounts to special customers.
I'd find it hard to give you any more.	There's more left.
You're bankrupting me!	This could be my best deal so far this year.
There are only crumbs left in the cupboard.	There's more to give.
It's not our usual policy to give discounts.	I can make an exception for you.

Some of these quotations are theatrical but still provide a strong message. Listen to what is exactly being said and choose your reply carefully.

THIS IS MY FINAL OFFER!

This is one statement that has to be taken most seriously. By definition there can be only one final offer. Once you have uttered these words, therefore, you should be very certain that you mean them.

If ever you move on a 'final offer' your credibility is torn to shreds. Nothing you can say subsequently can have any value if the other party know that there are several versions of 'final offer'. If you are negotiating with a person who moves from any form of final position be assured that this person is someone whose words cannot be taken seriously.

From a buying perspective very rarely ask for anybody's final offer. If they give it and it's not enough, what can you do?

IRRITATORS

It often pays to tape-record your own voice to see if there are any individual words or phrases that you repeat continuously or that when used may cause offence.

Too many 'y'knows' at the end of sentences can readily stop people wishing to listen to you. Calling someone 'my good man' or 'darling', for example, is likely to cause offence and be wholly counter-productive. In some instances legal ramifications may even ensue.

Telling somebody that this is the 'deal of the century' is not likely to endear either you or the deal to them. Make your language appropriate both professionally and socially.

Lastly, one should avoid clichés and jargon. These often create antagonism and such phrases as 'touching base with customers' and 'running ideas up the flag pole to see who salutes them' make most people shudder with embarrassment.

STEP 16   KEY POINTS

1. Check every written word carefully, especially when the document has legal consequences.
2. Listen for the real meaning behind the words.
3. Try to talk and think at the same time.
4. Don't use words like 'final' unless you really mean them.
5. Don't use offensive language and avoid clichés.

Negotiation Scripts

Which of the following scripts are useful and positive? Which should be avoided? Suggest reasons why and then compare your ideas with ours.

1. I'm sure we can sort something out on the delivery issue. It's only a small matter.

2. OK. Let's just check what we mean by 'free packaging and delivery'.

3. Look, I've given you 6 per cent already. I can't go very much more than that.

4. This is my final offer. I'm afraid it's all I can do.

OUR VIEW

1. Don't be fooled into thinking that anything in a negotiation is 'only a small matter'. You must be on your guard and if these words are used to you be aware that there could be a sting in the detail. From your view this is a fine way of moving the topic away from something that is to your disadvantage.

2. This is the antidote to 1 above. It puts you in control and shows that you're aware of the variables and want everything checked to your satisfaction.

3. This is where the experts score over novices. The key words are 'not very much more.' This does not mean that nothing is possible. That is a naïve perception. The real meaning is that there is plenty of money on the table. Your task is to obtain it. ASK AND YOU MIGHT GET IT!

4. Well, is it final or not? If you have said these words then you should make sure that it is. If these words are used on you then you should test to see if it really is. Try silence and see if the other party go into 'argument dilution'.

Tactics and Counterplays

You need to be aware of the tricks of the trade. Use them at your discretion but above all be aware of when they are being used on you!

- **You know what I mean**
  Let the other party interpret your words in their own way. It's their prerogative.

- **Last chance and final offers**
  Try to get the other party to move from a 'final' offer. It will be a good opportunity for you to test their skill and experience.

- **I beg your pardon**
  Don't be afraid to interrupt immediately if the other party seem to have made a verbal error, especially one in their favour.

- **Do we or don't we?**
  Check the negatives in the terms and conditions. Unscrupulous negotiators can easily omit a 'not' or change a date.

- **Darlings and mates**
  Don't be prickled if you are the victim of poorly chosen language.

Exercises

We all know exercises are important. They keep you fit and ready to negotiate. Think of real examples and try to relate our theory back to your own experience.

1. Write down three phrases that you can use to gain some negotiation leverage next time you're in a conversation.

2. Think of your most recent negotiations. Can you remember any words or phrases that you now know would have given you some extra, unintentioned information? Do any of your regular business colleagues have any pet phrases?

Negotiation Dilemmas

Here is an opportunity to test your knowledge against a set of difficult scenarios. What would you do in these situations? You can read our ideas after you have written your own.

Dilemma 32

You have just managed to extract movement from the other party on a 'final' position. What do you do as a result of this?

OUR VIEW

Good negotiators never show triumph and you shouldn't here even though you have secured a substantial strategic advantage in the negotiation.

You now know that the other party will move from a 'final' offer. This means that if they will move from one 'final' offer then they are likely to move from the next one and the next one after that. This is one of the small pieces of knowledge gleaned during a negotiation that allow you to build up a picture of both the nature of the deal and, more importantly, the other person.

Your next move will be to test the other party. Now that you know that they may be more able to move than you perhaps suspected you can probe areas of opportunity. These will centre on the major variables of the negotiation.

You have been conditioned by this one poor piece of behaviour to assume that much more movement may be possible than first thought. This reveals how vulnerable you become if you allow the other party to believe that you have more to give away.

Thinking in real time is important. Never say anything unconsidered that may come back to haunt you.

Negotiation Dilemmas

Here is an opportunity to test your knowledge against a set of difficult scenarios. What would you do in these situations? You can read our ideas after you have written your own.

Dilemma 33

The negotiator opposite insists that he has exceeded his limits and will need to call his boss for further advice. How do you react?

OUR VIEW

This could be both good news and bad. The good news is that you now know that the real decision maker is back at the office. You know that the person you are dealing with does not have total authority.

You could try to discover the identity of the decision maker and deal direct. This could be advantageous if you feel that the person with whom you are negotiating is really too junior for you to be able to reach a proper conclusion. This may, however, lead to antagonism between the other party and yourself if they feel that they are being undermined. You could destroy the relationship if they feel that they are undervalued.

The bad news might be that this is merely a ploy by a skilful negotiator to buy some space in the negotiation. He might need some time for thinking or extra planning.

It might be that the other side intend to use the 'boss' character as a lever against you. 'My boss won't let me go any higher' allows the other negotiator to remain your 'friend' and directs your unhappiness towards the boss. It is amazing in these situations how often the boss is unavailable for meetings with you. Should this occur you can use both emotion and logic to undo the tactic. Feelings of being 'let down` by the other party or perhaps a need to send more information to the boss by fax can start to unpick it. Ultimately this is often a ploy and you should treat it as such.

The best way, of course, is to ascertain the extent of the other party's authority at the start of the negotiation.

Just Before you Finish

List up to three things that you intend to do differently as a result of this step.

1.

2.

3.

Step 17   Looking like you mean it

The nature of communication has often been examined by experts and the following statistics are commonly quoted concerning the different ways in which communication takes place:

- 55% non verbal
- 38% tone of voice
- 7% words.

These figures reveal that non-verbal signals are very important.

Many good books have been written on the subject of body language and what seems to be particularly important is the manner in which body language matches your words and tone of voice. When you are able to combine all three elements, the point you wish to make is the more greatly emphasized and the other party are left in no doubt about your intentions.

A good example is when you wish to stress the importance of a subject. The choice of strong words such as 'This is nowhere near what I'm looking for' combines with a powerful tone of voice and gestures to add even more weight. Good eye contact and the use of the hands to push home the point will tell the other party that you mean business without antagonizing them.

CONGRUENCE

You must ensure at all times that your tone, words and body language are congruent. They must add value to your ideas and not detract from your argument. There is little point in making a good point if your voice is quiet and you are sitting with arms and legs crossed looking thoroughly defensive. You must ensure that the words 'fit the music'.

INCREASING NON-VERBAL LEVERAGE

Some elements of non-verbal communication are particularly important in negotiating. The following points are those that every expert negotiator should know and use.

1. Eye contact
The importance of eye contact can never be underestimated. It is one of the most important means by which humans communicate. You must avoid looking away at a key moment. When the words are loaded with emphasis, eye contact will give them even more impact.

As children we are taught not to stare, and some people find too much eye contact threatening.

Salespeople are often advised not to wear tinted lenses if they wear spectacles. The customers need to see their eyes. Would you buy double glazing from a salesman wearing sunglasses?

2. Body position

Always try to sit up to a table with your arms on the table. If you place your hands in your lap it will stop you using your hands to emphasize a point and will also prevent you from taking notes.

3. Smile and nod

This is a classic listening posture. It will encourage the other party to continue talking and will make you seem engaged in the business. This is particularly important when you are negotiating in a team and one of your colleagues is talking.

4. Be a mirror

A very subtle technique which helps create rapport with the other side is to try to mirror their gestures and also to listen to their words. Check for any particular word that seems a favourite which you can then return to them at a key moment.

Be careful not to cause offence. If mirroring is done well it helps to cement a bond of trust across the table from which good deals will flow.

THE POWER OF 'YES'

'Yes' is a very powerful word. It shows agreement and allows the other party to feel that you are both on the same wavelength.

If you do not agree with the other side try to find some way of saying so that will not make them feel threatened. Remember, the more that they like you and feel at ease with you the better chance you have of obtaining movement from them.

A powerful alternative word here is 'interesting'. It says that you will develop the idea without suggesting that you agree with it.

Good words to suggest disagreement are 'incomplete', 'needing an adjustment', 'almost concur with you but', 'heading in the same direction'.

STEP 17   KEY POINTS

1. Make sure that your tone of voice fits the words and that your words are backed up by assertive gestures.
2. Maintain good eye contact, have a positive posture and be a friendly audience.
3. Try to reflect back to the other party the tone, words and gestures they are using to you. Make them feel at ease when dealing with you.

Negotiation Scripts

Which of the following scripts are useful and positive? Which should be avoided? Suggest reasons why and then compare your ideas with ours.

1. I can see that you seem perturbed by what I'm saying.

2. Mr Williams, your argument is incomplete. Have you thought of the consequences of a large price rise?

3. Let's both work together here. I'd like your support.

4. That's an interesting point, let me just come back to you with a question, if I may.

5. That's a most interesting proposition. I think that with adjustment we might be able to get somewhere.

OUR VIEW

1. You've noticed that the other party is ill at ease. Use this knowledge to obtain their dissatisfaction from them before the issue gets worse. Never be afraid to discuss feelings in a negotiation.
2. You are saying that you thoroughly disagree but you have found a way of putting it so that the other party doesn't feel threatened and doesn't feel that you are a hostile adversary.
3. Come and join me. Appeal to their emotion and show that you are both on the same side and are seeing the issue from a similar viewpoint. Good way to create rapport.
4. This is a holding comment. You may have been given a very difficult statement and you need some thinking time. This type of expression keeps the atmosphere warm and at the same time allows you to come back with some comments.
5. Very polite and friendly but hiding the fact that you disagree with what they said and believe it ought to be revised. Excellent use of vocabulary.

Tactics and Counterplays

You need to be aware of the tricks of the trade. Use them at your discretion but above all be aware of when they are being used on you!

- **I'm in charge**
  Don't be put off by power handshakes and aggressive behaviour. Most of this is a sham designed to put you on the defensive.

- **Let me ask you a question**
  If you find the other person leading you with a battery of questions break the sequence. Don't allow yourself to be taken on the 'yes, you're right' path.

- **Let's be friends**
  Make a conscious effort to create rapport with the other party. Follow their words and gestures and try to agree with what they are saying as far as is professionally permissible.

- **I'm not sure that I agree**
  'Yes, but' is more powerful than 'No'.

- **Do you really like me?**
  Be careful if you find the other party agreeing with you too readily. What do they *really* think?

Exercises

We all know exercises are important. They keep you fit and ready to negotiate. Think of real examples and try to relate our theory back to your own experience.

1. Write down three things that you can do to encourage the other party to feel at ease with you in a negotiation.

2. Find three ways of disagreeing with somebody without it seeming that you do.

Negotiation Dilemmas

Here is an opportunity to test your knowledge against a set of difficult scenarios. What would you do in these situations? You can read our ideas after you have written your own.

Dilemma 34

You notice that the other party are trying to copy your gestures and have just repeated back to you one of your pet expressions. How might you react?

OUR VIEW

It is one thing to know the theory, it is clearly another to implement it skilfully. You're up against somebody who has read the theory but is 'obvious' when putting it into practice.

A quiet inward smile may be the best approach here. There is little point in creating friction when it is not best suited. You could try putting your hands behind your head, linking your fingers and leaning back. It will be interesting to see if the other party mimic that gesture. You could 'mirror' the other party by copying phrases yourself and then repeating to them something that they have just used. Touché.

You may well use this approach to see if the other party know any other tactics or ploys. Certainly if you find any of them being used offensively you can return the comment or gesture with interest.

Be careful that nobody could ever have the same problem with you.

Negotiation Dilemmas

Here is an opportunity to test your knowledge against a set of difficult scenarios. What would you do in these situations? You can read our ideas after you have written your own.

Dilemma 35

You shake hands with a new salesperson and notice that they are hesitant, have a weak handshake and will not look you in the eye. What thoughts should be occurring to you?

OUR VIEW

This is the opposite problem. It would be very surprising if any salesperson were to behave in this fashion as the majority will have either received training on this point or understood the principles as a matter of common sense.

If this is a true cluster of gestures you are obviously dealing with somebody who has little confidence and perhaps not a great deal of negotiation horsepower. Your expectations will rise and you may wish to test your assumptions concerning your targets. This could be good news.

What you must guard against if you are dealing with a novice or somebody who is not skilful is being greedy or over-confident and dominant. Remember that the majority of people you meet in business are people that you will have to meet again.

There is no mileage in milking a deal and finding that the other party cannot live with the consequences (this could cost you money in the long run). Equally there is no point in taking advantage of a novice negotiator to the degree that they feel humiliated and resentful. Again this could cause problems in the long run.

This situation requires a subtle softly-softly approach.

Just Before you Finish

List up to three things that you intend to do differently as a result of this step.

1.

2.

3.

Step 18   When the going gets tough

Expert negotiators are a phlegmatic group of people. They are normally in control of their emotions and only show that part of their feelings that is most likely to produce results.

There is little room for a short temper in a negotiation. The ability to sit and smile (both outwardly and inwardly) allows the negotiator the opportunity to think and plan without jumping to conclusions.

When necessary negotiators can become angry and upset, or laugh when amused *but each time they are fully in control.*

PRIDE

Without doubt the most destructive emotion within the negotiating room is pride. This causes buyers to refuse a great deal and sellers to look elsewhere for a customer. If you want the other side to hate you just hurt their pride and watch the results.

Pride and ego need to be massaged rather than brutalized. A principal theme of this book is the need to build strong, personal relationships with fellow negotiators. If you wish to do this it will increase their sense of personal and professional pride.

THE DEFEND/ATTACK SPIRAL

Non-expert negotiators have a habit of wanting to hit back when attacked. This causes the other side to do no more than increase the attack. The result is usually a totally destructive environment where emotion becomes so strong that a good outcome for the negotiation becomes a secondary objective.

If the other party wishes to `get you' at all costs then you must roll with the punches and not hit back with unfavourable comment unless you have clearly thought through the consequences.

CHECK THE TEMPERATURE

Constantly check the personal temperature of the negotiation. If you find the discussion becoming heated and unproductive it is correct to intervene and admit it. Use words such as 'I can see we are getting a little heated here.

Why don't we take a short break and come back in better shape in ten minutes?'

Expert negotiators are always in control but are similarly always ready to admit their feelings openly. You will be more respected if you are prepared to open up about your feelings rather than sit there seething with anger.

APOLOGIZING

If you wish to keep the temperature of the negotiation at a reasonable level it is good practice to apologize with good grace whenever there is a breakdown of the process or if emotions are getting too high.

Two particularly powerful ways to apologize without losing any advantage are to use the words: 'Problem' and 'Misunderstanding'. Learn expressions like 'I'm sorry that there has been a misunderstanding here' and 'I do apologize for this problem.' Neither of these phrases point the finger of blame and they can be used freely without damaging credibility. There may be many reasons why the misunderstanding or problem occurred. The important thing is to get it resolved and move on to more productive issues.

STEP 18 KEY POINTS

1. Keep inward control of your emotions.
2. Don't needle the other negotiator.
3. Don't enter into a defend/attack spiral – unless planned.
4. Manage the personal temperature in the room.
5. Be prepared to admit your own emotions when necessary.
6. Apologize if necessary.

Negotiation Scripts

Which of the following scripts are useful and positive? Which should be avoided? Suggest reasons why and then compare your ideas with ours.

1. It's always a pleasure to visit your factory.

2. I'm sorry if that sounded a bit blunt, but sometimes there's no other way to put it.

3. Can I interrupt a moment, please. I'm beginning to feel a little frustrated here and I think it's important that we sort this out.

4. I can see you're beginning to get a bit annoyed. Why don't we take a short break. It will do us both good.

5. I can see why you're so passionate about this but really we must approach the matter with a little more control, don't you think?

6. I think there's been a misunderstanding here. I'm sorry this has happened. Let's see how we can resolve it.

OUR VIEW

1. Why not start the meeting with a pleasantry. You shouldn't be too keen to get down to business and a comment like this at the beginning helps start things off in a warm and friendly manner even if you are facing a tough meeting.
2. You know that you must reject an offer but that does not mean that you cannot treat people with respect. A balance between being rigorous with the deal but courteous with the people is needed.
3. You've performed two excellent behaviours. First, you have interrupted properly and, second, you have not been embarrassed to tell the other party about your feelings. Comments like this usually prove useful.
4. Much the same here except that you have spotted it with the other party and you are trying to prevent an escalation of any problem.
5. The other party may be losing their temper and you are trying to maintain some control without antagonizing them. This is a difficult situation and if you can perform this successfully you will defuse any hostility before it becomes destructive.
6. Excellent language to get you out of a difficult situation leading to a quest for resolution by both parties.

Tactics and Counterplays

You need to be aware of the tricks of the trade. Use them at your discretion but above all be aware of when they are being used on you!

- **Mr Nice and Mr Nasty** (again)
  The classic play on emotions is the 'Mr Nice, Mr Nasty' ploy. Don't be taken in when one member of the team opposite seems to be unduly hostile while another tries to be more accommodating.

- **It's only a game**
  Some negotiators will purposely try to upset you so that you lose control for a moment or become side-tracked by your feelings. Remember that negotiation at this stage is only a game and you should treat it accordingly.

- **It could be worse (Russian Front)-** (again because it's important)
  Don't be taken to the 'Russian Front!' Some negotiators will present such a hostile and difficult set of circumstances that when you do achieve something that looks reasonable you will settle for it because in comparison it seems good. Don't be misled by comparing everything with the worst case scenario. Why not compare it with the best case?

Exercises

We all know exercises are important. They keep you fit and ready to negotiate. Think of real examples and try to relate our theory back to your own experience.

1. Who is your most emotional negotiation adversary? Is there any way in which you can use their volubility to your advantage?

2. Who are most likely to use emotion in a negotiation, buyers or sellers? What evidence or examples do you have for this?

Negotiation Dilemmas

Here is an opportunity to test your knowledge against a set of difficult scenarios. What would you do in these situations? You can read our ideas after you have written your own.

Dilemma 36

Your counterpart across the table suddenly loses their temper and becomes most unpleasant. What options do you have and how can you exploit the situation to your advantage?

OUR VIEW

When this happens in a negotiation the one thing to keep in mind is the absolute need not to get angry (unless planned). You should not allow the other party to put you off by their bad behaviour.

With your control maintained you act firmly and assertively. In a quiet manner you can look the other party in the eyes, smile in a friendly way and make it very clear that their behaviour is not going to cause you to move on any major negotiation variables.

Choose words such as 'I can see that you're very passionate about this issue, but I must say that it doesn't shake me from my commitment that . . .'

You might be a little firmer with something like 'I'm sorry to have to say that I'm finding this negotiation to be a bit too heated for my taste. Why don't we take a break for ten minutes . . .' You then get up and make it clear that you are taking the break even if the other party do not agree.

At each stage make it clear that you are not going to be a soft touch and that bullying tactics will not work. If you are presented with inappropriate language then you have every right to make it plain (in a firm and friendly manner) that you would prefer if such language wasn't used.

Make your point without raising the temperature of the negotiation.

Negotiation Dilemmas

Here is an opportunity to test your knowledge against a set of difficult scenarios. What would you do in these situations? You can read our ideas after you have written your own.

Dilemma 37

The woman leading the purchasing team against you looks at you and says 'This is getting us nowhere. I'm feeling frustrated and it looks like this afternoon has been a complete waste of time. Give us what we want or we'll just have to leave.' How do you reply and what actions should you take?

OUR VIEW

Good negotiators know that they should not make threats unless they are prepared to carry them out. You have been clearly threatened and the question you must ask yourself is whether you wish to call their bluff and, if so, will they really walk out.

When someone is behaving threateningly, one way of dealing with it is by an unexpected response. It is a way of side-stepping the issue and giving you time to reduce the temperature in a potentially explosive situation while still retaining your integrity.

In this instance you could agree with some part of what was said, for instance, 'Yes, I can see that you are becoming frustrated and that you think that this afternoon is a waste of time!'

The word 'yes' can often take the other party by surprise and put the brakes on. You are not actually agreeing with what they say only that you can see that they believe what they said.

There may well be more to the statement than meets the eye. It might be a tactic and if so your follow up could be 'We certainly do not wish it to end like this. Let's look at the possibilities that would be best for all.' If this does not alter their approach and a walk out is inevitable you must make sure that they understand that you believe their behaviour is counter productive and unacceptable.

As previously discussed if you reward bad behaviour then you will only receive more bad behaviour. Be honest and let the other party know that you will not give in to their blackmail and that you find the whole situation unpleasant and even unprofessional. Of course, you must phrase this in a quiet, assertive manner and ensure that the temperature is kept down.

Just Before you Finish

List up to three things that you intend to do differently as a result of this step.

1.

2.

3.

Step 19   Emergency!

Occasionally the wheels can start to come off during a negotiation. Nothing ever goes wholly to plan. It is, therefore, just as well to plan for the unexpected.

PLAN B - THE 'WHAT IF' SCENARIO

The expert negotiator has always planned well. You can call that Plan A. This is the intended course of action and should always be fully researched and ready to roll. For the more important negotiations you also need a second set of plans. These are the contingencies that you planned and prepared in Step 4 and will come in to play should anything go awry in Plan A. This, then, is Plan B.

You should always be asking yourself 'what if' every time you plan. There will be a whole range of alternatives by way of responses and you should be ready for them. Your Plan B is your safety net if the unexpected happens. Ask yourself these two questions:

- How can I prevent things from going wrong?
- If things do go wrong how can I get out with minimum pain?

With these two principles in mind you should be able to plan for most problems and have a reasonable course of action ready.

DON'T SIT AND SUFFER

If you find that the flow of the negotiation is against you and that the other side have grabbed the advantage and are making it tell, then do something. There is absolutely nothing to be gained by sitting and allowing the opposition to score points.

- You can recess.
- You can visit the toilet.
- You can try to bring lunch forward.

All of these represent actions that will be better than sitting and suffering. They may not work but they will prove to be better than doing nothing. Slow the process down and during a recess list questions that you could ask. Ask the other party to repeat the point they are making – again and again.

YOU CAN'T ARGUE WITH COMPUTERS

Walking into a negotiation with a portable PC can be a real advantage. It offers a major piece of one-upmanship but more tellingly allows you to 'run the software' at crucial moments to create some breathing space. This, of course, can take as long as you wish and can break the flow of the opposition while at the same time offering some validity for the decision you subsequently make ('you can't argue with the computer').

Similar use can be made of a calculator and any other props that may come to hand. But be very careful about making calculations in a meeting!

STEP 19   KEY POINTS

1. Be aware when the negotiation is going against you. Do something about it.
2. Do your 'what if' planning. Have a range of contingency plans and be prepared for the unexpected.
3. Don't sit there and be hypnotized. Do something to break the flow/slow things down.
4. There's always time for another meeting. Take an adjournment and put another date in the diary.

Negotiation Scripts

Which of the following scripts are useful and positive? Which should be avoided? Suggest reasons why and then compare your ideas with ours.

1. It's getting very hot in here. Do you think we could open the windows and get the air conditioning sorted out?

2. That's a good point. I was thinking about that just the other day. I reckon the approach for your new proposal could be . . .

3. I'm sorry to interrupt you, but my boss asked me to call at 3 o'clock. Do you mind if we take a short break?

4. I'm going to need to sort that out with our finance people. Why don't we meet next week and I can give you a definitive answer.

OUR VIEW

1. Why be uncomfortable? It could be coincidence or it could be that the other party have organized it like that. Either way be politely assertive and get the environment changed.
2. You can make new suggestions. You may be able to derail the other side because they do not have a Plan B.
3. It's difficult to say no. It's the polite way to get a timeout or report back to base.
4. Better to get the numbers checked rather than make a miscalculation on the spot. There's always time for another meeting.

Tactics and Counterplays

You need to be aware of the tricks of the trade. Use them at your discretion but above all be aware of when they are being used on you!

- **Group therapy**
  In team negotiations be careful of caucus discussions in the toilet or over lunch. You can be excluded from important ideas when separated into smaller groups.

- **The non commercial novice**
  Watch the engineers in your team. They are notoriously prone to giving away key points at crucial times. The technical members of the team must be as well trained as the commercial people when it comes to a team negotiation.

- **Time management**
  If the other side wishes to delay the flow with a ploy, leave the room. Being asked to sit idly while they make a call or crunch some numbers gives them the advantage. Use this as a chance to freshen up and collect your thoughts out of the room.

- **Walk this way**
  Be careful of the walk from reception up to the office. At this early, unguarded moment important information can often be unwittingly given away.

Exercises

We all know exercises are important. They keep you fit and ready to negotiate. Think of real examples and try to relate our theory back to your own experience.

1. Write down three things that you can do to ensure that you don't get pushed into a difficult position too quickly without being prepared.

2. Whose agenda do you use in a negotiation? Think of your last three negotiations. Who took control? Who was doing the leading?

Negotiation Dilemmas

Here is an opportunity to test your knowledge against a set of difficult scenarios. What would you do in these situations? You can read our ideas after you have written your own.

Dilemma 38

What is your reaction to the negotiator opposite who keeps being interrupted on their mobile phone?

OUR VIEW

If you are going to be charitable you might assume that the person opposite is merely unthinkingly being discourteous. If this is the case then you can politely inform them that the telephone is causing a great deal of disruption and as time is short could they please switch it off.

If, on the other hand, you feel that this is merely a tactic being used against you, you might just wait a while and let the scenario unfold. If the other party is trying too hard it might be worth sitting back to admire the cabaret but at the same time be very aware of what is taking place so that you can use it to your advantage.

Be aware that all tactics can be used unskilfully.

Negotiation Dilemmas

Here is an opportunity to test your knowledge against a set of difficult scenarios. What would you do in these situations? You can read our ideas after you have written your own.

Dilemma 39
Nothing is going to plan. You have completely miscalculated what was needed. How can you survive and retain credibility?

OUR VIEW

Is honesty the best policy? What will do the least harm to your credibility? There are several considerations.

If you already have an established working relationship with the other party then you can afford to be upfront with your apology and you know that you have enough history between you for business to continue. Things do occasionally go wrong and in this particular scenario you should say so.

It is slightly different if you are meeting somebody for the first time or if the business or personal relationships are not so well established. If you own up to an error or a miscalculation or just rank bad organization you must ask whether honesty will be better than bluff.

Damage is likely to be done whatever the situation. How you handle it depends on a variety of tactical circumstances. There may also be a moral element here.

You must be guardian of your own morals. Be honest or try to bluff, take a chance and risk being embarrassed later. The choice is yours!

Just Before you Finish

List up to three things that you intend to do differently as a result of this step.

1.

2.

3.

Step 20   The long run

If you have got as far as Step 20 you must now be feeling that you have started to understand some of the ways in which expert negotiators behave and some methods of improving your own style. This step is by way of revision and contains just a few core ideas which could stand you in good stead in the long run.

LEARN TO BE DISSATISFIED

Expert negotiators are never satisfied. They are perpetually concerned by the possibility that they have left money on the table. As we have discussed earlier you will never *know* how near to the edge of the cliff you were. That is the joy or the pain of negotiating.

You should always walk away from a negotiation with a feeling that you could have got more. 'I wonder if he would have given me an extra 1 per cent if I had pushed him harder' are the words that should be in your head. If you leave a negotiation smiling with the thought that you have had a good result just ask yourself if you really pushed as hard as you could. Did you go for the "Wow!?"

We are not suggesting that negotiators are a breed of malcontents. Your thoughts should be towards obtaining the highest levels that are available. Be a keen, friendly negotiator with high targets.

BE PERSISTENT

Expert negotiators do not readily take 'no' for an answer. They will check it out, ask you to validate your ideas, revisit your evidence, question you again and then they might start to think that 'no' is a faint possibility.

'If you don't ask you don't get' is a well worn cliché but despite sounding trite it is a major theme for negotiators.

One of the main elements of this workbook is the need for an expert negotiator to 'keep at it' and not roll over too readily.

WARM AND TOUGH

This section is devoted to a small graphic which summarizes many of the key points in the 20 steps.

An expert negotiator needs to look at two different aspects of a negotiation: the task at hand and the people involved – the business and the personal dimensions (see also Figure 2.5). The combination that has stood the test of time is to be tough on the deal and warm towards the people. Graphically it can be represented as shown in Figure 7.1. The tick represents the preferred style area. This style is rigorous on the numbers and the money but friendly towards the people.

Unfortunately far too many negotiators adopt a cold/tough attitude. This will achieve deals but by no means the quality of deals that a warmer approach would achieve.

Sales people are usually quite different. Many of them are so afraid that they will lose the deal that they adopt a warm/easy approach. This gains them the sale but never really puts money on the bottom line.

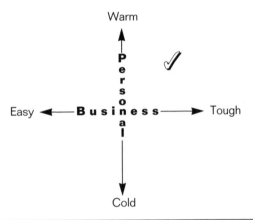

Figure 7.1 The balanced negotiator

SOME LAST THOUGHTS AND TIPS

Here is a last list of those tactics and techniques that we would most readily recommend. It will help focus your mind on the key issues at the end of our learning process.

We often go wrong in negotiation, not because we have been doing something badly, but because we have not been doing something we should have done, or because we have been doing something we should never have done. If you can remember and action the do's and don'ts in this section, you will eliminate the negative and develop the positive.

The list of do's and don'ts is not exhaustive. It aims to get those who negotiate to think about the process. To quote Oliver Goldsmith:

> For just experience tells, in every walk of life,
> that those that think must govern those that toil.

Negotiation – Some Do's

- Dig in, early on, on a big issue and stick close to your position.
  The effort of doing so begins to alter the other party's expectation of the final deal that is to be struck. 'Happier with less'.
- Work out the relative bargaining powers of yourself and the other party.
  If you have power, use it carefully and gently at first. Take care that if you use power to get your own way, then sooner or later they will do the same with you – perhaps on the next deal. You will have taught them how to deal with you.
- Try to get into a position where you don't have to use the bargaining mode of negotiation.
  Never betray by the merest gesture that you are willing to trade. Take a posture and stick to it as long as possible.
- Trade or bargain on the 'straw' issues.
  If you have to trade do so only in the minor issues (straw). Make these issues appear important, for example by only trading them and never giving them away. Go through the motions of bargaining and allow the other party to 'win' concessions.
- The scout's motto: 'Be prepared'.
  Preparation and planning is important. We never have enough time. However, there is generally no difference in the time allocated to this phase of negotiation by average and successful negotiators. The difference is in the type of planning. Successful negotiators balance their time between process (how) and task (what) issues rather than concentrating on task issues only.
- Stage manage your team.
  If you are not alone then allocate tasks:
  – calculations
  – tracking concessions
  – opportunities.
  Avoid at all costs the person who hasn't been *Listening* and jumps in with both feet to undermine your case.
- Make the other party compete.
  Avoid premature commitment to their product or service. Keep them selling because their propensity to make concessions will be greater.

Hiding the true quantity you want to buy is another way of making them compete. Selectivity and variation in timing of purchase will also help.

- Recess.
  Use this tactic to avoid the early close or premature pressure to commit. To consider/review difficult issues and to make even the shortest of calculations – especially when a calculator is involved. Never feel bad about it. Time the recess to maximum effect.

- Integrity rather than complete openness.
  Good negotiators do not reveal their total hand, nor do they tell the complete story of what they want or why they want it. Good negotiators reveal information in small pieces, as and when it is necessary. They hide from their opponents feelings about the objectives they have been set to achieve. Having said that, they must provide an anchor for the other party. If they make a commitment it has to hold. If the other party distrust the negotiator they will be nervous/anxious and may withdraw. They will almost certainly become more difficult to deal with. **A good negotiator must be trustworthy.**

- Listen, rather than talk.
  We are all inclined to waffle and wave the flag; we keep talking to show what good negotiators we are and to display our knowledge. If we lack confidence it helps to keep up our spirits. How wrong we are. It pays much more to listen. Listening and responding to the other party helps create empathy. The listener will be able to spot opportunities, detect problems, judge the limits of the other party's position and, when they do talk, they will do so with more knowledge. Hence increasing their confidence and ability to ask good questions.

- Summarize.
  Do so regularly not just at the end. Sum up the points you like and weaken your opponent's position by ignoring or playing down those you don't like. Use it to illustrate the concessions you need – 'If you can do this and this, then we . . .'

- Lend a helping hand.
  If the other party get themselves into a deep hole it can pay well, on occasions, to give them a ladder. A small investment for a larger return.

- Aim high.
  The more you ask for the more you get. It pays to make high demands. However, a posture must be credible. Too high, and you will achieve deadlock or the other party may withdraw. Very high demands need to be tentatively signalled to the other party in order to test reaction and set up expectations. Price lists are one method used by sellers to condition buyers to low expectation or to give a predictable response.

- Authority.
  Ensure that you understand the levels and extent of your authority in the

areas in which you are to negotiate. The tactic of 'removed authority' or 'defence in depth', that is removing or strictly limiting authority, can be beneficial if not declared to the other party.

Negotiation – Some Don'ts

- Don't make things easy for the other party.
  People derive more satisfaction from things they have worked hard to get. Give the other party this satisfaction. On the other hand at the end make it a *little* better than they thought it was going to be.
- Don't compromise early in the meeting.
  Compromise will favour the party who postures most extremely. Use it to break an impasse or bridge a 'last gap'.
- Don't always leave the important issues to the middle/end of the agenda.
  To do so is the predictable behaviour of the average negotiator. Often this results in lack of time for the important issues.
- Never, ever, show triumph.
  The sting in the tail. We have all seen the negotiator who lost and said little, but seethed with anger and determined to beat the other party, if not destroy them, the next time.
- Don't feel too successful.
  Bernard Shaw once said 'Success is the brand on the brow of the person who aimed too low.' Are we successful? Was our need to feel successful strong? Was our perception of what was possible lowered?
- Don't 'paint' yourself or the other party into a corner.
  Leave yourself room. Good negotiators don't use 'either, or', they use 'if and then'. A cornered animal can be dangerous. Never ask:
  - What is your lowest price?
  - Is that the best you can do?
- Don't go it alone on protracted or complex negotiations.
  To negotiate and remain objective is very difficult. To have a partner who remains objective can be beneficial. Besides the obvious benefit of increased security, another person can, for example:
  - decide when a recess is relevant
  - plot concessions made by the parties
  - listen and watch for signals – sometimes what is not said rather than what is said.
- Don't lack confidence.
  Those who have confidence will ask questions/get information and challenge positions and ideas. Why does one lack confidence? This arises from two related yet somewhat different sources:

– The fear of losing.

– The fear of facing an experienced opponent.

Both can be avoided by knowledge: preparing your groundwork thoroughly and knowing that you are a trained, skilled negotiator. Lack of confidence often results from fear that a mistake might be made. It is a pity because we learn more from our mistakes. Remember, the making of a mistake is not a final defeat – it can be rectified without damage to one's negotiating position.

- Don't get side-tracked.

The use of side issues is a classical tactical ploy. Don't wander, unless you intend to do so. The other party will try to side-track you if they consider they are losing a particular point under discussion or that a telling point is about to be made against them. Be on your guard! The 'backburner' is a useful counter-tactic.

- Don't be greedy.

A negotiator needs to push hard then grab that result/opportunity and not try for something the other party will never give. Being greedy risks losing all. Don't take that risk.

- Don't move quickly.

A slow concession pattern is a trait of a good negotiator. Go for the most you can get and don't move from this top limit of your aspirations too easily. To do anything else signals an initial demand that was too strong and motivates your opponent to push you down.

CONCLUSION

You have now worked through 20 steps. You may have been an expert before starting this work, in which case you will have picked up some tips to make you even more effective. You will have checked out your style and can feel a little more comfortable about your strategy and tactics.

If you started out as something less than an expert you will have learnt a little about what an expert does but more importantly you should have an understanding of how an expert thinks and feels. This is what will really help you in the long run.

The last thought of the book is this: if you don't use it, you'll lose it. Now that your confidence is high go and practise. Try a car boot sale, a street market; try a hotel or two over the telephone. The worst they can say is 'no'. You might actually enjoy it!

INDEX